Giuliana Ferrini

In the same
INTERNATIONAL
FILM GUIDE SERIES
edited by Peter Cowie

HOLLYWOOD IN THE THIRTIES

by
JOHN BAXTER

TANTIVY PRESS, LONDON
A. S. BARNES & CO., NEW YORK

Acknowledgements

THE AUTHOR wishes to thank the following groups and individuals without whose assistance this book would not have been possible: Eric Thompson, Chris Collier, Paramount Pictures Ltd., Metro-Goldwyn-Mayer Ltd., Charles Gilbert and Graham Stone of the Australian National Library (Film Division), Ian Klava, Barrie Pattison, Bill Collins, Douglas White, David Stratton, Josef von Sternberg, and Miss Barbara Wronowski.

The special assistance of Mr. Charles Higham is also acknowledged. Portions of this book originally appeared in FILM DIGEST magazine, and are reprinted by permission of the Editorial Board.

All dates, spelling, etc are based on the *Catalogue of Copyright Entries: Motion Pictures 1912-1939*. (Library of Congress, Washington, D.C. 1951.)

Front Cover: Jean Harlow in *Dinner at Eight.*
Back Cover: (Thirties) Spencer Tracy in *Twenty Thousand Years in Sing Sing;* (Twenties) Rudolph Valentino practises the tango; (Forties) Joan Crawford in *Mildred Pierce.*

Contents

FOR MY MOTHER . . .

who told me about Lupe Velez.

"There are two Hollywoods; the Hollywood where people live and work, and the Hollywood which lives in the mind of the public like a fabulous legend. Before we can understand the movie colony we must understand its legend; and before we can understand the legend we must glance at a few facts. . . ."

Leo C. Rosten
HOLLYWOOD: The Movie Colony,
The Movie Makers

1. The Fabulous Legend

ON NEW Year's Eve, 1929, it was raining in New York, but the streets were still full. The theatres were packed as if there had never been a depression; the memories of 1929 and of the big slump were fading. People who had once preferred to stay home were coming out, filling the hotels and smart restaurants.

On Broadway, one could see Alfred Lunt and Lynn Fontanne in their newest drama, or "Bitter Sweet", a play by the latest rage, Noël Coward. For those not able to afford the price of a theatre seat, there were movies, including Helen Morgan in *Applause*. With sound a commonplace now, and colour, the simple two-colour Technicolor that enlivened sequences of many musicals, widely used, the movies were better than ever.

Two thousand miles away, in Los Angeles, they thought that too. As the film-makers of Hollywood gathered to celebrate the new year, the directors, producers and stars in one group, the technicians and lesser actors in another, one felt a sense of relief in the gaiety. It had been tough for a while. The crash had hit a lot of people in the West as well. Sound had brought problems, and ruined many. Some familiar faces were gone, back to Europe perhaps where their voices were not the bar to employment that short-sighted producers had made them in America.

Replacing the actors who had been driven out by sound was a new kind of people; directors and technicians from Germany and Austria, cameramen from Budapest, set designers from Prague. And mixed in with them were new American faces; flamboyant actors from Broadway, speaking a new jargon and wearing their unaccustomed wealth like a gaudy jewel. There were playwrights too, directors from New York, designers and hangers-on, all brought in to satisfy the demand for the sophisticated feeling of the stage which producers imagined sound films would demand. The old residents were nervous but willing to try the new thing. It wouldn't be too bad, and perhaps sound had something. They would work at it. They would have to.

In New York the crowds came out of the theatres into the rainy streets. "The New York Times" for January 1st, 1930, was already on the stands, its editorial bright with confidence and the assurance of great names. In Hollywood, the parties became noisier, the groups blended, coalesced; somebody began to sing "Auld Lang Syne". Like the actinic blooming of an arc light, the Thirties began.

★   ★   ★

Of all periods in the history of the cinema, none is more important to its growth and perfection as that of Hollywood in the Thirties. In the decade between the Great Depression and the Second World War, American society suffered its most sweeping changes since the Civil War, changes which were mirrored and distorted by the popular arts, and especially by the cinema. In 1929, the cinema had explored, despite the work of the German expressionists and the early American masters, only a part of its potential. Notwithstanding the great beauty of some late silent films, many techniques, not only those of sound, were at this time primitive and clumsy. Acting and writing for films with few exceptions drew inspiration only from the stage. Film needed the stimulus of a disordered and slightly hysterical period to discover its true potential, as its first great advances had been made under the complex social pressures of Germany after the First World War.

Ten years after the coming of sound, cinema had progressed, despite setbacks and sidetracks, to an incontestable position as the greatest of the popular arts. Hollywood's combination of almost unlimited capital and professional expertise had developed for the first time a completely efficient system for the production of motion pictures. Through a ruinously expensive but finally profitable policy of purchasing the best talent, no matter where it came from, it had built up a community of film-makers containing the finest minds ever to apply themselves to the cinema. Prodigal, decadent, wasteful, Hollywood was at the same time ruthless in its pursuit of excellence in the film-making process. The result of this policy was a national cinema which, for richness of invention, has never been equalled. Greater film-makers than some of those in

Hollywood could and did exist in other countries at the same time, but for sheer concentration of genius and imagination, Hollywood in the Thirties had no equal.

Among the first points to strike any researcher into the American cinema of the Thirties is the inability of modern critical theory to cope with the bulk and nature of the material. We have come over the last few years to accept the premise that film is a director's art, and that the true cinematic creator exhibits in all his work a vision which binds it into a cohesive statement. While this theory is undoubtedly applicable to such film-makers as Resnais and Antonioni, writer/directors whose total output of features adds up to less than a dozen each, it becomes ludicrous when applied to men whose careers span thirty years, and whose scores of films, written, produced and occasionally partly directed by others, provide a mass of material in which the search for a connecting vision and intellectual consistency becomes both futile and irrelevant. Michael Curtiz made 44 films between 1930 and 1939, Mervyn LeRoy 36, John Ford 26. No genius could function without variation under such pressure.

There is no inflexible rule for allocating measures of blame and praise in films of the period, but the presence in Hollywood of hundreds of major film artists, most of whom contributed to many films other than those they directed, argues against the applicability of the *auteur* theory or any variation of it. A few directors, of course, had a greater share in the making of their films than others; the most important of these have received the attention they merit in Chapters 6 and 7, "The Great Originals". But while films have been grouped throughout the book under directors, this system has been adopted as much for convenience as for any other reason. The inclusion in the personalities studied of cameramen, set designers, producers and other technicians should indicate that there can be little doubt film-making in Hollywood during the Thirties was very much a group activity contributed to by many creators under the general supervision of a director.

The key concept of Hollywood films and especially of Hollywood in the Thirties is that of the studio. Without the studios, Hollywood could never have existed. An understanding of the studio system and of the financial and organisational processes on which it was based is central to any examination of the period. In its hothouse atmosphere were bred the worst excesses of Hollywood and its greatest glories. Not one of these organisations is unworthy of serious study, but there is space in this book to deal in detail with only three of them, Metro-Goldwyn-Mayer, Paramount and Warner Brothers. From these three concentrations of talent, a large percentage of the best Hollywood films have come.

Although the studio was primarily an economic convenience, its effect on the artistic aspect of film production was marked. In fact, the commercial and artistic histories of Hollywood are inextricably interwoven. While it may have become the movie capital of the world for reasons as apparently irrelevant as its clear weather, proximity to Mexico and safety from legal pursuit, Hollywood's continued existence depended entirely on the supply of money from reputable sources of capital — banks and established corporations. Their support depended in turn on the continued growth and stability of the film industry. In the early days of the cinema, films were made by independent distributors and then sold by them to exhibitors at whatever price they could fetch, but this was a system offering small profits and scant security. The moment when a producer decided that the process was both unwieldy and risky and looked around for an alternative method of distribution marked also the birth of the studio system.

First step in the welding of the system was the film exchange, owners of which would purchase or lease films from producers and rent them out to the popular "nickelodeons". Soon, enterprising exhibitors, most of whom had had experience in the ruthless world of burlesque and vaudeville, founded their own exchanges to ensure a cheap and regular supply of films. Among the first people to see the possibilities of this monopolistic enterprise were men like Marcus Loew and William Fox, both of whom left the chancy fur and garment trade in Chicago to buy in on nickelodeon chains. Four brothers named Warner left their early training in salesmanship and in the bicycle trade to make a similar purchase, as did garment manufacturer Carl Laemmle. By the late 1910s, the nickelodeons had become theatres, the exchanges mere clearing houses for the supply of films to the proprietors' chains of movie houses.

The next stage was obvious. Further to guarantee their business, the exchange/movie-house owners had to control the amount and content of film produced. The exhibitors, though mainly New York based, began to explore the possibility of extending their holdings among the film studios in California and Long Island. Slowly, through a complex and often illegal series of purchases and takeovers, exhibitors entered into partnerships with the larger producers of films. Loew's theatres amalgamated with the Metro studios and Samuel Goldwyn, Carl Laemmle acquired Universal, the Warner Brothers Vitaphone and First National, William Fox the studios which bear his name. By the middle Twenties, film production had become linked to film distribution.

It would have been very easy for the studio system to be a stultifying force in the cinema, paralysing the imaginative and encouraging the mediocre. In some studios, this occurred; Columbia seldom managed to struggle out from under the control of "King" Cohn, its inflexible, tasteless boss, while in others, a consciously contrived studio "look" forced all directors into the same stylistic mould. Elegant as the early Paramount movies are and fast-paced as one finds those of Warners in the Thirties, one often wishes their directors had been allowed to pay more attention to the material and less to the orders of the "front office".

Each studio had its team of technicians, and it is these teams that dictated to a large extent the look and sound of American films. Its art department, working under a supervising art director who seldom did more than block out the general lines of a project and approve the completed drawings, employed dozens of draughtsmen and designers, each of them working on a small part of the overall plan. There were specialists in interiors, exteriors, ships, castles, nightclubs, Oriental buildings; a film requiring some or all of these would involve the talents of ten men, each making a major contribution which would receive no acknowledgement in the film's credits. The credit to Cedric Gibbons on almost all of Metro's major films of the Thirties and Forties indicates only that Gibbons, admittedly a great designer, exercised a supervisory control over the designs. Where a credit is shared, it often means that he relinquished this control to another designer, who himself organised the team. There are notable exceptions, but in almost all cases film design was a group activity.

In photography, more individuality was possible. The great lighting cameramen were professionals of such high qualification that few of their fellow workers were competent to correct their set-ups, and as a result they left their mark on the films they shot to a greater extent than did art directors, editors or any other technician. It is significant that the greatest films were made when director and cameraman established an understanding strong enough for them to work together towards a desired effect. William Wyler and Gregg Toland, Clarence Brown and William Daniels, the much vexed duo of Josef von Sternberg and Lee Garmes; these teams produced the great visual adventures of the period.

Beyond the bright area of the major credits, the studio system becomes a shadowy maze, some relationships remaining forever obscure. The creative contribution of the scriptwriter is in some cases, as in that where directors also collaborated on the script, fairly clear, but in general it is impossible to discover who wrote what. The section in a later chapter on *Gone With The Wind* should indicate as well as anything how confused such matters could become. The function of the editor is also difficult to define. Great editors did exist, and where their work is distinguishable from other technicians they have been recognised. In general, however, it has not been possible to single them out. Their work is no less great because of this. The failure to acknowledge it is just one result of the cinema's ill-documented and purposely obscurantist history.

A devotion to stereotypes has falsified much of our attitude to the studio system. The popular image of the Hollywood producer is that of an obese, cigar-chewing vulgarian interested only in profit, that of the director a monocled neurotic in jodphurs and riding boots thwacking his thigh with a riding crop and screaming in broken English. A survey taken in the late Thirties, however, indicated that 57% of working Hollywood producers had a university education, while the corresponding figure for directors and assistant directors was 53% and 55% respectively. For writers, the proportion was a notable 80%. The influx during the early Thirties of cultured artists and technicians from the studios of Europe added a cosmopolitan sophistication to the film-making colony, combining with the natural talent of the American film-makers to give Hollywood's cultural community an intellectual climate well above that of the average university town. It is arguable, in fact, that Hollywood during the Thirties and Forties contained one of the highest concentrations of intellect and sophistication which America has seen.

It is to the intelligence of the Thirties' film-makers that we owe the shape of the cinema today, its general debility and occasional glories. Their experiments during the early days of sound film were, for all their intellectual bravura, devoted mainly to finding the perfect equation for commercial cinema, and in this they succeeded. The Hollywood product of pre-1935 is most interesting precisely because they had not then perfected their techniques. There was still room for the technical exercise and intellectual statement which made late silent films intermittently brilliant. As the Thirties proceed, however, one senses a codifying and restraining influence at work, categorising subjects, "typing" stars, and destined eventually to present us with the strictly compartmented cinema of the Forties, with its "women's pictures", "actioners" and "prestige productions". What the Forties gain in technique, they lose in content; yet, paradoxically, when the Thirties were at their most intellectually brilliant, they did not have the technique to capitalise on it. What Hollywood gives with one hand, it almost always takes away with the other.

13

The centrality of the studio system to any understanding of American films during the Thirties has dictated to some extent the form of this book. A chapter has been devoted to each of the major studios, while later sections deal with directors who worked outside the system and technicians who did not become directors but nevertheless made a major contribution to the period.

Many omissions have been dictated by the limits of space. Among the first films to be discarded, with regret, were animated productions, documentaries and short films, even though many of them are important. The "March of Time" and "Crime Does Not Pay" Series are among the most interesting products of Hollywood, as is the work of Walt Disney. The sorrowful deletion has also been made of almost all the "B" films of the period and of such studios as Monogram and Tiffany, on the assumption that similar generalisations can be made about these films as about their more expensive contemporaries. A further, and perhaps more important omission, has been the work of directors who seem to have made their best films in the Forties and later. Nobody will contest the skill of Raoul Walsh and Allan Dwan, but the success of their later work makes it both unjust and unkind to estimate their overall importance on the basis of these earlier efforts.

It is implicit in the approach of this book that no critical line is imposed on the material, but a writer would fail in his function if he did not make clear to his readers the basic beliefs behind his attitude. These will, of course, become apparent to the reader as he progresses, but an early warning is no more than courteous.

I believe that, between the years 1929 and 1935, the cinema was remade, and remade for the better. The American cinema has always been the world's most inventive, the source from which all others have derived their key ideas, and its renaissance meant, inevitably, that films from every country of the world would change as a result. The early promise of Hollywood has been betrayed, and the American cinema has never been able to sustain the quality of the films produced during its richest period of invention. Despite this, the films of the Thirties remain incomparable exercises in artistic creation.

The second emphasis which readers will notice is a heavy one on the matter of technique. It is not fashionable to consider the way in which a film is made more important than the intent of the creator in presenting it, but no other view of the cinema seems to offer any hope of consistency. Anthony Burgess's remarks on James Joyce seem to sum up best of all my own attitude. "The glory and mystery of art," he says, "can lie in the tension between the appearance and reality, or, rather, between the subject-matter and what is made of it. The view that the subject-matter should be itself enlightening still persists, chiefly because a moral stock response comes more easily to most people than a genuine aesthetic transport." The truth of this summation seems as apparent in the cinema as it is in literature and art at large.

The description of the Thirties as a "Golden Age" of the American cinema is a common one, yet, despite its worth as an encapsulated critical response, it is far from satisfactory. Nor is there any "magic" about the Thirties. "Magic," James Thurber says, "is a word without sweat. Perfection, which achieves its end by labour, is better." Hollywood in the Thirties was a brutal, vulgar, grasping place, inhabited by people not especially devoted to any coherent artistic concept. And yet, somehow, they produced great art. How and why they did it — these are the subjects of this book.

2. The Studios: Metro-Goldwyn-Mayer

GREATEST OF all the studios was Metro-Goldwyn-Mayer. It was the richest, the biggest, the most productive. Tied to the extensive theatre chain of Marcus Loew, it had access to the largest film outlet in the world, while its financial associations with the Chase National Bank gave it capital so extensive that no production, however elaborate, was a risk. At its peak, the twenty-two stages of Metro and its hundred acre back-lot of standing sets produced forty-two feature films a year, the biggest output of any studio in the history of the cinema.

Controller of Metro throughout the Thirties was Louis B. Mayer, ex-ragpicker, nickelodeon owner, then an independent producer and distributor of films. From 1924, when Loew's Inc. bought out Samuel Goldwyn's Goldwyn Pictures Corporation and then hired Mayer and his associates Irving Thalberg and Robert Rubin to control the production side of this huge film-making/film-distributing organisation. Mayer had unlimited power not only over Metro but, by virtue of the studio's influence and prestige, over the entire American cinema. Paradoxically, it was a power he was ill-fitted to use. An astute and ruthless businessman, Mayer was no artist, and it is generally accepted that only the young Thalberg during his tenure as Metro's executive in charge of production was able to keep the studio's films at their high artistic level.

However it was done, the standard remained constant. Metro's films had a polish and a technical virtuosity that is uncontested in the period. There is a brightly lit, sharp-edged intensity that conveys the spirit of the country and period, as did its roster of female stars — Garbo, Shearer, Harlow, Crawford, Rainer, Loy. Under the great design director Cedric Gibbons, Metro's sets achieved a verisimilitude and elegance of proportion few studios or individuals have matched. Douglas Shearer, its pioneering sound engineer, did more to perfect recording for films than any man, just as his sister, Norma Shearer,

"*Undoubtedly the most inventive of Metro's directors*": Clarence Brown (below, right) directed ANNA CHRISTIE (right) with George Marion, Greta Garbo and Charles Bickford; and A FREE SOUL (below, left) with Clark Gable and Norma Shearer.

A notable Metro director was W. S. Van Dyke (top, left) who directed the early films in THE THIN MAN series which starred William Powell, Myrna Loy and a pet called Asta who frequently diverted attention from the stars (above, right); he was also responsible for one of the studio's biggest hits, SAN FRANCISCO, which starred Clark Gable and Jeanette MacDonald (left)

became the first of the stars genuinely to grasp the realities of acting for sound cinema. Metro's dress designer, Gilbert Adrian, set a clean, smoothly draped style for gowns that now seems pure Thirties, while its cameramen — William Daniels, Karl Freund, Harold Rosson, George Folsey among them — developed the brilliant high-key lighting still looked on as the ideal.

It was, however, in its contract directors that Metro had an edge on almost every studio. Thalberg's adventurous, if quirky talent encouraged many complex projects, while the money Metro could pay allowed him to hire men capable of carrying them out. Over the late Twenties, the Metro team of directors became both strong and diverse, made up of men willing and able to specialise but also adaptable to Thalberg's unusual ideas. Undoubtedly the most inventive of these was **CLARENCE BROWN.**

Older and more experienced than most of his Metro colleagues, Brown had come to the studio with a complex background in business, as assistant to the great European director Maurice Tourneur in the 1910s and early Twenties, and some reputation as a producer. After directing *The Eagle* (1925) with Valentino, he bought the rights to the original story of *The Unholy Three*, which Metro had wanted, and sold it to them at a huge profit, causing Thalberg to swear Brown would never work for Metro. Eventually, he was to become their top director, the man trusted with Garbo, a prestige artist who could be indulged with a leisurely schedule of one picture a year. His films of American life, and especially his celebrations of the nation's rural virtues — *Ah, Wilderness!*, *The Yearling* — are among the most beautiful and true things ever put on film, though it is paradoxical that he should have become most famous for stagey dramas featuring the difficult and temperamental Greta Garbo.

Anna Christie (1930) was Greta Garbo's first sound film and one of the first of Metro's productions to establish the studio as the major force of the Thirties. With *Flesh and The Devil* (1927), Brown and cameraman William Daniels set the Garbo style that was to become her insignia — the high-arched brows and lofty forehead bared by

17

swept-back hair, a face burned into white by high-key lighting so that the strong, almost masculine bone structure was forced out. Daniels, eventually to become Garbo's cameraman as Brown was her director, lit *Anna Christie* with an intensity that partially betrayed the gloomy nature of Eugene O'Neill's intramural tragedy, but his work makes it a distinctive film and one of the most striking of the decade's first years.

Despite an accent thicker than even modern filmgoers are used to, Garbo is memorable as the unlucky ex-prostitute whose past catches up with her just as she is about to marry. The climax where, her temper lost at last with her drunken, weeping father (George Marion) and blustering Irish lover (Charles Bickford), she reveals the degradation of her life on the farm to which the former has sent her, her rape by one of the farmer's sons, and descent to a midwestern brothel, is a *tour de force*. Ranting, shouting, muttering in almost broken English, she holds one's attention totally. A notable *mise en scène* — dockside water like black oil, rotting piles and foggy lanes, the echo of a tinny piano — culminates in a remarkable sequence; as the drama is finally resolved, Marion goes to the door and, looking out, muses on the complexities of life. "The fog . . for a while you can't see where you're going. Then it lifts . . .". The final shot is a brief one of the sea, terrifyingly grey and wind-whipped under a low sky, an image of Melvillian drama and the powerful end to a mixed, occasionally brilliant film.

Anna Christie is not Brown's greatest film of the early Thirties, though it is the best of the half-dozen Garbo vehicles he directed. He seemed better able to work without the tyranny of Garbo's talent and the restrained style her stiff, intense acting imposed on him, which may account for the effectiveness of the Garbo-less *A Free Soul* (1931). The story, a paltry melodrama about a drunken but brilliant attorney (Lionel Barrymore) and his sensitive independent daughter (Norma Shearer), earned the year's Oscar for Barrymore, though one doubts that any performance in the film could have been worthy of an award had not Brown scraped through the surface of the script to find the genuine drama of Adela Rogers St. John's original story, based on

18

her own early life and that of her father, the Los Angeles lawyer Earl Rogers.

Barrymore seems mannered today — like Wallace Beery, another top Metro star, he had only one portrait in him, a crude caricature of himself — but Shearer, by contrast, is superb. Striking rather than beautiful, her ferocious squint neatly camouflaged by Brown, she wears Adrian's gowns with the erotic flair that a lack of underwear could inspire. Only Jean Harlow was able more effectively to suggest nudity beneath the draped silk. Shearer's casual *déshabillé* in the film's early shots, where she dresses in her father's apartment after a night on the town, prepares us for her romance with Ace Wilfong (Clark Gable), a racketeer whom Barrymore saves from a murder charge and who immediately involves Shearer in a torrid affair.

Her first visit to Gable's apartment is meticulously directed. She wanders around, stretching, lounging, unable to resist, even if she had wanted to, his crudely broadcast desire. He kisses her, and though she says coolly, "That will be all, thank you," it is obvious that she is hooked. "A new kind of man," she murmurs a little later, "a new kind of world." Later scenes exhibit her frank sexual hunger. Arriving at his apartment, she throws herself down on the couch, and putting her arms out to Gable, says, "Cummon, put 'em around me." Though the film degenerates later, with Shearer's ex-fiancée (Leslie Howard) murdering Gable, then being saved by a drunken Barrymore, who drops dead at the end of his speech to the jury, nothing can detract from the intensity of its early scenes, nor from Shearer's magnificent picture of arrogant female sensuality.

The middle Thirties saw Brown occupied with more Garbo vehicles, including such well-known productions as *Anna Karenina* (1935) and the wordy *Conquest* (*Marie Walewska*) (1937), the latter notable mainly for Karl Freund's soft lighting which gave Garbo a new femininity not popular with her devotees. He also achieved in *Ah, Wilderness!* (1935) a far more effective adaptation of Eugene O'Neill than in *Anna Christie*. This was his first excursion into the field of Americana which was later to inspire his best films. Despite the qualities of *Ah, Wilderness!*, how-

19

ever, Brown's greatest and probably most under-rated film is a later and even more perceptive entry into the same area, the remarkable *Of Human Hearts* (1938).

Acting performances dignify and enlarge this story of a young boy, son of a poor country parson, growing up in an Ohio village before the Civil War. As the minister, Walter Huston brings to the film a dignity and sense of form which it could not otherwise have achieved, while Beulah Bondi as his resigned wife is perfectly cast. Charles Coburn's drunken doctor, an energetic performance from James Stewart as the son, Clyde de Vinna's excellent exterior camerawork; these qualities, combined with Bradbury Foote's script, make this one of the Thirties' great films.

Of Human Hearts perfectly re-creates the period. Huston's parson is a striking combination of peasant strength and religious fanaticism. The family's arrival in the village, the meanness of the townsfolk who, slyly pleading hard times, cheat them, are brilliantly realised, as is their surprise at Huston's willingness to endure their parsimony, the sarcasm of the blessing which he offers up, thanking the Lord that he has only a small family, going over their heads. The tension between ambitious son and stern father is built up skilfully, culminating in a darkly violent scene where Stewart defies Huston during a trip into the mountains, punches him, then stops, terrified at what he has done, standing dumbly as Huston beats him mercilessly to the ground. A tethered horse rears frantically behind them, recalling, perhaps symbolically, an earlier scene in which Huston, the personification of strength and prophet-like majesty, catches and takes for his own a white horse that has run wild through the village. The final scenes of *Of Human Hearts* dissolve, as do those of *A Free Soul*, into sentiment, but the Civil War background and Stewart's believable portrayal of a talented but thoughtless young doctor do much to make this Brown's most consistent film.

Brown was the embodiment of canny 19th century rural America. His films reflect a passionate but controlled response to people and places; the suspicion and foresight which have made him today a rich man show themselves in his work. Like Whitman, he hears America singing; but he does not choose to sing himself.

Metro's most prolific director was **W. S. "WOODY" VAN DYKE II.** Brown had a wide formal education—Van Dyke came to films via jobs as a gold-miner, lumberjack and actor. Brown considered his films carefully, constructing them with an essayist's feel for balance—"One Shot Woody" produced 32 features from 1930 to 1939 and worked on a number of others, shooting all of them with great flair and skill but little polish.

Van Dyke's films do not lend themselves to consideration singly. He was an expert with series pictures: *The Thin Man* (1934), *After The Thin Man* (1936) and *Another Thin Man* (1939) are all competent excursions into the genre of light comedy-drama so effectively mastered by Michael Curtiz at Warners around the same time, while *Trader Horn* (1931) and *Tarzan, The Ape Man* (1932) are "African" films. Van Dyke also did two of the Andy Hardy series, with Mickey Rooney, but *It's A Wonderful World* and *Andy Hardy Gets Spring Fever* (both 1939) are inferior to those made by George B. Seitz (see Chapter 9), while his Nelson Eddy/Jeanette MacDonald vehicles *Naughty Marietta* (1935), *Rose Marie* (1936) and *Sweethearts* (1938) did little to counteract the reaction against the duo in sophisticated circles while it led to their being christened "The Singing Capon" and "The Iron Butterfly."

Occasionally, Van Dyke was able to break away from the formula picture to create a genuinely individual film. One of these was *The Devil Is A Sissy* (1936), starring the usually emetic Freddy Bartholomew, a seasoned Mickey Rooney in possibly his best role of the Thirties, and a variety of Metro contract players. The film probably owes its qualities, however, to Rowland Brown, the brilliant scenarist/director who wrote the original story and who in fact began directing the film. The story is about a child (Bartholomew) of divorce who lives half of each year with a socialite mother and half with a struggling architect father in the slums of New York, and the observation of behaviour among

21

slum kids and the mechanics of social acceptance in this complex environment is remarkably apt. Occasionally the script takes flight, as where Rooney struggles through the days after his father is electrocuted for murder, refusing to break down but coming perilously close to the unforgivable indignity of tears on more than one occasion, especially when, standing under the harsh glare of a streetlight, he hears the clock chime the hour of execution. Next day, however, he can boast that "it took three jolts to kill him", and dignity is saved. There is a grisly scene where a boy, aptly named "Bugs", eats an ant ("I ate a butterfly once . . . its wings tasted all dusty . . .") and another reveals a genuine six-toed foot. The picture of slum life is accurate without criticism, funny without sentiment, and Van Dyke's direction is, as always assured.

Van Dyke's greatest success was the sprawling *San Francisco* (1936), an ambitious epic culminating in one of the finest of the period's special effects, a strikingly re-created San Francisco earthquake. Clark Gable, playing a Barbary Coast saloon owner patterned on gambler/wit Wilson Mizner, moves through the evolutions of a love/hate affair with dance-hall-girl-cum-opera-singer Jeanette MacDonald (here kept firmly in check by the director), undisturbed by Spencer Tracy's gloomy priest and unshaken in his dedication to easy living until the earthquake brings him to his senses. In one of her best scripts, Anita Loos makes use of the rich American urban mythology to construct memorable sequences; a noisy concert stopped by MacDonald with a spirited rendition of the song "San Francisco", crisp verbal duels between Gable and rival Jack Holt, MacDonald appearing modestly draped in a veil to sing at Tracy's service, the brawling, vivid Barbary Coast streets — but everything stops with the earthquake, a magnificently staged cataclysm to which Van Dyke's direction builds up with fast-tempo editing of trembling ceilings and clashing chandeliers. The final sequence, where a battered but unbroken population strides back, to the tune of "The Battle Hymn of the Republic", into the ruined city, is sentimental, but few can resist its triumphant chauvinism. Intellectually disreputable though his films may have been, Van Dyke had no equal as a studio technician and as an estimator of popular taste.

Though a better director than Van Dyke, **SAM WOOD** did not make his mark until late in his career, when during the Forties he made such masterpieces as *Kings Row* and *Ivy*. In the Thirties, however, he was one of Metro's top men. Already an experienced technician in the 1900s he was assistant to DeMille for some time, and embarked during the Twenties on a directorial career which, though largely undistinguished, does exhibit unexpected moments of genius. His handling of the nihilistic Marx Brothers in *A Night At The Opera* (1935) and *A Day At The Races* (1937) is impeccable, perhaps because unlike others he does not neglect the supporting cast or the intervening musical and romantic sequences which Irving Thalberg considered necessary to the films' commercial success. Under Wood's direction, the Marx set-pieces do not come as high-points in a dull landscape but arise naturally from the smooth fabric of the film. Hilarious though the Marx Brothers are, in fact, it is sometimes other scenes one remembers, like Sig Rumann's kissing of Margaret Dumont's hand in *A Night At The Opera* which metamorphoses briefly into a greedy examination of her diamond rings. In *Goodbye Mr. Chips*, and *Raffles* (both 1939) Wood was similarly sure in his handling of fairly conventional material, but it is regrettable that the Thirties work of this undoubtedly superior director should have been distinguished mainly by its succession of competent but routine films.

In the work of **SIDNEY FRANKLIN**, it is possible to see what Sam Wood might have been had he been handed more complex and prestigious assignments. In 1929, Franklin made a successful adaptation of a pet Thalberg project, the Broadway hit *The Last of Mrs. Cheyney*, with Norma Shearer, which led to him being typed as a director of "prestige pictures". During the Thirties he was to be given a substantial number of Metro's stage adaptations, including *The Guardsman* (1931) and *The Barretts of Wimpole Street* (1934), but none which he was to transpose so successfully as Noël Coward's *Private Lives* (1931).

However unfaithful to Coward this adaptation may be, *Private Lives* embodies at least the spirit of the playwright and his time. As Amanda and Elyot, divorcees who meet again on the night of their second marriages and realise they have always been in love, Norma Shearer and

Robert Montgomery are superb. Cool, desperate to be uncommitted but frequently slipping, they convince completely, especially in the famous balcony scene where, first with bitterness then returning passion, they review their marriage and the meaninglessness of their lives since its ending. Coward's malicious wit comes out in all their exchanges, however, and is allowed free rein in the second half of the film, where the runaway lovers are tracked down in their Swiss chalet by their legal spouses (Reginald Denny and Una Merkel) who are then demolished at an hilarious breakfast confrontation. Franklin is deft in his handling of this essentially four-cornered conversational comedy, beyond criticism in his direction of dialogue. For polish, few comedies of the Thirties can equal this early alliance of cinema and stage.

Franklin's handling of *The Guardsman* (1931) was less competent, though circumstances throughout made this a difficult film. Never entirely free of the Hollywood belief that sound film required people with stage training, Thalberg had wanted to bring to films the top Broadway team of Alfred Lunt and Lynn Fontanne, and eventually was able, with the help of Robert Rubin, to sign them for a screen version of their hit play, "The Guardsman". Though the film was financially successful, the studio's reverence for its distinguished stars shows through continually. In addition, the Lunts' doubt as to their ability effectively to work for the screen was not unfounded. The Ferenc Molnar story, involving a jealous actor who impersonates one of his wife's admirers to test her fidelity, functioned well on stage, but its static form — to establish the principals' situation, the film opens with a long excerpt from the Lunt success "Elizabeth the Queen" — made it heavy going. Only Lunt's unfilmic but arrestingly physical acting style is completely successful, as illustrated by an early shot where, with back to camera, he mutters, from "Hamlet", the line, "Oh, that this too too solid flesh would melt" and appears to wilt under the strain of his fatigue.

Franklin's undoubted masterpiece of the Thirties, however, was *The Good Earth* (1937), though it is difficult to discover in this instance the degree to which the film was his. Begun by the ill-starred George Hill (see Chapter 9), who died after having spent some time in China collecting background material, the project was handed to Victor Fleming, who in turn was forced by ill-health to call in Franklin. Few films made by Metro can have involved more talent. The original Pearl Buck novel was worked on for almost two years by Frances Marion (George Hill's wife), Talbot Jennings and Tess Slesinger, but Franklin told Kevin Brownlow that he regarded this first script as "too occidental" and wrote the final screenplay with Claudine West alone. Hill, Thalberg and others had been contemplating the project since 1933. The two Oscars it earned— Luise Rainer, best actress; Karl Freund, best camerawork—have given it an official standing, but its artistic worth is less sure.

Some of *The Good Earth* is admittedly magnificent. Like Mervyn LeRoy's *Oil for the Lamps Of China*, it attempts to re-create the history of China's last generation with reference to a single group of people, in this case, a young farmer and his family. Wang, the farmer (Paul Muni), takes his wife (Rainer) from the rich house where she is a slave, gains her trust, establishes himself as a landowner and, despite famine and other setbacks, becomes rich. When revolution breaks out and he is in danger, Rainer saves him, but he is diverted by a dancer (Tilly Losch), whom he takes as a second wife.

This film is one of the superb visual adventures of the period. The aggressively bare Chinese landscape, with its mathematically precise fields and neat huts, is perfectly re-created, as is the smooth-face impassivity of the people. The clean-swept feeling of the images and the uncluttered performances give credibility to the simple story, and contrast effectively with the occasional moments of fantasy — Tilly Losch's dance at the festival, her almost animal face and bizarre costume making her, as she was in Richard Boleslavski's *The Garden of Allah*, an embodiment of lust and decadence; the incredible arrival of a locust plague, or the revolutionary riots, with Rainer escaping a firing squad to flee through an orgy of destruction in which the world seems to be crumbling under surging masses of people. Even in these scenes, however, the film's main theme, that of the importance of the land, is not lost, though it reaches its greatest intensity where, in an especially horrible scene, the family is forced during a famine to eat earth. Flawed by its simple-mindedness and deficient in some supporting performances, *The Good Earth* is nevertheless a striking and original film.

In 1938, Franklin was, at Mayer's order, taken off active direction to become a producer. This unfortunate decision, part of the general confusion at Metro after Thalberg's death in 1936, meant the ruin of what had been a major project, *Marie Antoinette* (1938), which, though planned by Franklin, was completed by Van Dyke with expedition but little else. It was not the first time Mayer had quashed what might have been a great film. In 1934, he had interfered with the production of the curious and complex *Viva Villa!* (1934), eventually to be released over the signature of **JACK CONWAY**.

Conway, yet another actor turned director and one-time assistant to Griffith, is an interesting artist whose work has received little attention. One can only wonder how much greater his reputation would be today had he been allowed to complete *Viva Villa!*. With Wallace Beery as Villa and begun on location in Mexico with Howard Hawks initially as its director, the film even as it now stands has a power not often encountered in action melodramas of the time. Beery plays Villa as a simple-minded romantic, childlike and almost stupidly patriotic but capable also of insane frenzies when angered. It is a compelling performance, convincing because it is probably close to Beery's own character. *Viva Villa!* is a strange poem of violence; ragged groups of cavalry surge out of dust clouds like avenging ghosts or stand impassive around a doomed man; a murder is suggested by the movement of a boy out of a lighted door into a shadowed street to follow the footsteps of his victim; in a final sequence, at the climax of his victory, the bandit strips and flogs a beautiful aristocrat in a frenzied mutilation of that which he is brutishly unable to make his own. One will never know, however, what part of the film is Conway's, and what part Hawks's. In the middle of shooting, Hawks was called back to bear witness against actor Lee Tracy, who had allegedly made insulting remarks

26

about the Mexican army during the film's production. Conway, however, did the fine interiors, and it may be to his craftsmanship that it owes its power.

In character and skill, Conway and Hawks are similar. Both were men-about-town, card-players, party-goers, well-known for their sharp clothes and hectic social life. Conway was, in addition, a close associate of Thalberg; groomsman at his wedding, he was one of the two friends present when he died. Conway's films are, like those of Hawks, often concerned with the relationship between comrades, the necessity to "keep face" and retain one's masculine integrity. His direction of Ronald Colman in *A Tale of Two Cities* (1935) seems, because of the aptness of the Sydney Carton character to Conway's approach, especially effective; nobody has captured so accurately Carton's melancholy fatalism or the moral necessities which can drive a man to self-destruction. If only for the scene where Carton waits in the snow at Christmas time and watches the carollers and church-goers hurry past to the warmth of the home which he does not possess, *A Tale of Two Cities* must be considered one of the most successful films of the period.

Conway was also, however, a skilled comedy director. His direction of John and Lionel Barrymore in *Arsene Lupin* (1932) had, in addition to Conway's perceptive sketch of comradeship between rivals, a witty bite, as has one of his best later comedies, *Libeled Lady* (1936). This complicated situation comedy in which newspaper editor Spencer Tracy involves William Powell, Jean Harlow and Myrna Loy in a scheme to get him out of a libel suit brought by Loy is notable for some savage wisecracking from Harlow and a sequence in which Powell, ignorant of the art of fly fishing but lying frantically to his host Walter Connolly to the contrary, manages to catch a much-hunted trout. It is interesting to note that Hawks lifted this idea almost intact for his film *Man's Favorite Sport?* made some thirty years later.

Conway's funniest and most satirical comedy, however, is *Too Hot To Handle* (1938), in which Gable and Loy carry on a complex love-hate affair in a variety of locations from China to the Amazon jungles. Gable, cast to type as an unscrupulous and scheming newsreel camera-

27

man, is first seen manufacturing film of the Sino-Japanese War, initially by shooting at Japanese planes to bring on an air raid, then, when this fails, faking one with a well-paid Chinese child, a toy aeroplane and some artfully designed ruins. Loy, whose reputation is ruined by Gable in his search for a scoop, finally falls for him when he accompanies her to the Amazon to search for her lost brother, and rescues him after having dressed up as a witch-doctor. Breathlessly paced, witty and violent, this is one of the more acid comedies to have been produced by the Thirties.

VICTOR FLEMING shared with Conway the ability to impose on most of his films a distinctive style, but where Conway was fast, hard-hitting, witty, Fleming was, like William Wyler, contemplative and elegant. His films with frenetic players like Jean Harlow, such as *Bombshell* (1933) and *Reckless* (1935), are not among his most successful, though his skill at handling the essentially romantic material of *Captains Courageous* (1937) brought Spencer Tracy that year's Academy Award. An uncharacteristic example of a Fleming film in the Metro style is *Red Dust* (1932). This jungle drama is as false as others of its time, but its tense sexuality and the presence of Harlow and the skilled Mary Astor give it an intensity over which Fleming may have had little control. The Harlow/Gable love scenes develop, even in the severely cut prints generally available, a great deal of heat, an effect accentuated by Gable's unshaven masculinity and the ruttish sensuality of Harlow.

Despite the success of *Red Dust*, Fleming obviously preferred — and excelled in — the gentle and fantastic. *The Wizard of Oz* (1939) is one of the Thirties' most engaging films, in which the fantasy, never over-done, complements Judy Garland's gawky charm. One wonders today if the Oscars it received for best music and best song are really so well deserved, but the design and effects are impeccable. One experiences a genuine moment of shock as a tree comes to life to grasp Judy, and is charmed by the gaiety of Billie Burke's exhortation to "Follow the Yellow Brick Road" or the infectious rhythm of "We're Off To See The Wizard". Fantasy seldom transfers well to the screen, but Frank

Baum's simple vision seems to have achieved its perfect reincarnation in Fleming's film.

The last film of the Thirties to be signed by Fleming was also the last of the decade to be released under the Metro-Goldwyn-Mayer imprint. It is paradoxical, and perhaps typical of the era, that Fleming did not direct all of *Gone With The Wind* (1939), and that it was not strictly speaking a Metro film. The confusion about who directed this production, who photographed and wrote it, how it was made and why, will probably never see resolution. But it is incontestably the greatest and most impressive of all the films made in Hollywood during the Thirties, displaying in rich array all the faults of the time as well as its virtues. One wonders whether any other will ever equal it for scope and magnificent hokum.

The genesis of *Gone With The Wind* lies in Margaret Mitchell's sprawling novel, published in 1936. Over-written, diffuse, most of its characters unreal caricatures, the book has nevertheless an impact which made it a best-seller of the time. Mitchell's agent, realising its filmic possibilities, involved herself strenuously in the sale of the movie rights, which eventually went to independent producer David O. Selznick, for some time with Metro but having left in 1935 to found his own company, Selznick-International. The $50,000 he paid for the book seems ludicrous now, and was to become insignificant beside the eventual cost of the film.

After buying the book, Selznick, having signed an agreement with United Artists to release all his product through them until 1939, realised that to make the film as he wanted it, with Metro star Clark Gable as Rhett Butler, would not be possible until that year, as Loew's would never agree to let him have Gable for a film not to be released through their outlets. Selznick, biding his time, hired veteran script-writer Sidney Howard to do a treatment of the book and set about finding a girl to play the difficult role of Scarlett O'Hara. The story of how he first saw Vivien Leigh, illuminated by the glow of burning sets representing the destruction of Atlanta, seems, incredibly enough, to be true, but whatever the reasons for his choice, Selznick made an admirable decision. One doubts that even Katharine Hepburn, or Bette Davis, originally favourites for the part, could have done any better.

The start of filming on *Gone With The Wind* in 1938 seems to have been a signal for everything to go wrong. Ben Hecht has described how, after three weeks' shooting, Selznick characteristically announced he was dissatisfied with the script and hired Hecht for one week's work at $15,000 to rewrite, with him and Fleming, the whole screenplay. It was only in the middle of this week, with all three men exhausted, that somebody thought to return for reference to Howard's original treatment, long forgotten and its author now dead. Using this as a basis, Selznick, Hecht and Fleming rewrote the script, although the credit and Oscar went to Howard.

Fleming was not the first director to work on the film, and on a number of occasions three first units were shooting at once on widely separated locations. George Cukor had originally been signed for the job, but left, allegedly because of friction with Gable, who felt that Cukor, well-known as a "woman's director", was giving Leigh all the best shots. Whatever the truth of this, Cukor is known to have shot at least three sequences — the opening scenes of Vivien Leigh with the Tarleton brothers, that in which Leigh slaps the hysterical Butterfly McQueen when she returns during Melanie's childbirth, and the shooting of the Union soldier as he enters Tara and threatens Scarlett. Later, when Fleming collapsed during shooting, the film was completed by Sam Wood. The exact contribution of the cameramen involved — Ernest Haller, Ray Rennahan (who both received the Oscar), Joseph Ruttenberg, Wilfrid Cline and Lee Garmes — must, unfortunately, remain in doubt, as must the allocation of credit for the film's design, officially given to Lyle Wheeler and William Cameron Menzies, who received Oscars for it, though attributed by George Cukor to Hobart Erwin.

Whatever the precise share of responsibility must finally be, *Gone With The Wind* remains a remarkable film. The opening sequences, evoking the prosperity and elegance of the old South, have a grace and ease that is characteristic of Fleming at his best. Thomas Mitchell, gaily racing his horse across streams and fields to meet his daughter, Scarlett, in a green meadow, is an apt symbol of Southern aristocracy. Their subsequent conversation about the importance of the land and of their plantation Tara culminates in one of the film's most dramatic images: as they walk to the hill's brow at sunset, the camera rises slowly to show them silhouetted against an orange sky, framed by a tree's twisted trunk and limb, and below them in the valley, Tara's quiet serenity.

The feeling of grace and gentility is sustained with skill through the first half-hour. One remembers the Wilkes' party, people in costumes of grey, blue and white which harmonise with the sombre décor, the only contrast Rhett Butler in black suit and white spotted cravat. In the afternoon, the belles undress to sleep through the warm hours while negro maids fan them with whisks. In contrast to these muted scenes, the Atlanta bazaar is almost garish, though performances divert us from its brightness. Here is the newly widowed Scarlett, bouncing her black-bustled backside in time to the music, and eventually being "bought" by Butler with a contribution of $150 to "The Cause"; Melanie (Olivia de Havilland) nobly giving her wedding ring to the same collection, followed quickly by Scarlett, an act which encourages Butler to comment wryly, "I know how much that meant to *you*, Mrs. Hamilton." Then the waltz, with Leigh's black skirt whirling into the camera as the scandalised dancers look on.

So much of *Gone With The Wind* is brilliant that it is almost impossible to single out special sequences. Especially striking on the script level, however, is the scene where Leigh, drunk more with remorse than grief after the death of her second husband, is visited by Gable with a proposal. Mammy (Hattie McDaniel) knocks on her door to announce his arrival. "I *tol'* him you was prostrate with grief," she says as Leigh swigs on a bottle of *eau de cologne* to cover her breath and reels downstairs to where Gable, after having helped himself to a *boutonnière* from a crushed wreath on the floor, is awaiting her. His proposal of marriage is blunt and brief. Leigh objects to this, whereupon Gable, sinking to one knee, offers a memorably amusing declaration in which he claims that his concern has softened into "a deeper emotion." "Dare I name it?" he continues, "Can it be . . . love?" This scene, and its last shot of the couple kissing in the light of the shuttered parlour, is one of the best acted and written in the film.

Gone With The Wind was a fitting finale to the story of Metro-Goldwyn-Mayer in the Thirties. Beginning as a studio tied excessively to the concept of sound film as theatre-on-the-screen, it progressed with the help of its directorial and technical team to a position of eminence which few film-making organisations of any period could equal. It was the film-making machine par excellence, the embodiment of the American dream of perfect organisation without loss of individuality. Perhaps for this reason it found itself most comfortable with the simple melodrama and optimistic comedy which are characteristic of the United States. The lack of European talent in the Metro team undoubtedly had a great deal to do with the form of its films, but it is probably unfair to say that it meant any diminution in worth. Metro-Goldwyn-Mayer in the Thirties was American film-making at its best; unfortunately, it is only by a few people that this might be considered a compliment.

3. The Studios: Paramount

THERE WILL always be argument about the exact importance of Paramount in the history of Hollywood. It is considered by some researchers to have been the greatest of all studios, exceeding even Metro, but their evidence is sketchy. At some times during its history, and especially in the late Thirties when it cornered the market in light comedy drama, Paramount may well have been the most productive of Hollywood studios, but its constantly shifting financial structure

Wallace Beery was Pancho Villa in M-G-M's VIVA VILLA! Above right: Paul Muni and Luise Rainer starred in M-G-M's THE GOOD EARTH.

Stage stars Lynn Fontanne and Alfred Lunt made their only essay in the cinema for M-G-M: Sidney Franklin's THE GUARDSMAN.

"One of the Thirties' most engaging films . . ."
THE WIZARD OF OZ, directed by Victor
Fleming. Judy Garland's Dorothy comforts
the Cowardly Lion (Bert Lahr) watched by
the Tin Man (Jack Haley) and the Straw Man
(Ray Bolger).

GONE WITH THE WIND, a great achievement of the late Thirties: Rhett Butler (Clark
Gable) renews his acquaintance with the newly widowed Scarlett (Vivien Leigh) at the
Confederacy charity ball in Atlanta (opposite page); Ashley Wilkes (Leslie Howard) goes to
war, leaving behind Melanie (Olivia de Havilland) and Scarlett (below, top left); Rhett and
Scarlett's flight from the burning Atlanta (below, top right and bottom left); and the
Confederacy wounded filling the streets of the city (bottom right).

The seductive Ancaria (Joyzelle) confronts frightened Christian girl Mercia (Elissa Landi) in Cecil B. De-Mille's THE SIGN OF THE CROSS. Mitchell Leisen's imaginative costume design is seen to advantage.

"Décor in Paramount productions was never merely a background; settings insinuated themselves into the action". Warren William as Caesar and Claudette Colbert in the title role of DeMille's CLEOPATRA.

does not seem to indicate an organisation whose statements of profit may be looked on with any confidence. This situation of large parts of the studio bankroll being wagered on the success or failure of single productions seems to have been typical of Paramount in the Thirties, and is not indicative of a stability solid enough to make it a serious competitor of Metro.

Paramount was founded in 1914 by W. W. Hodkinson, a successful exhibitor of better-class motion pictures who wanted to break the monopolies even then growing up in the business. He offered independent film producers an opportunity to have their films released through a prestigious circuit of theatres in return for product of a high calibre. First of the many production companies to join the group were Adolph Zukor's Famous Players Co., and Jesse Lasky's Feature Play Co. Independent producer Samuel Goldfish became Chairman of the Board of Directors of the new company in 1916, but later left to become, under the name of Sam Goldwyn, a major producer in his own right. By the Twenties, Zukor was firmly in charge of the whole Paramount organisation. He retained a seat on the Paramount board most of his life, but he lost effective control of the company in 1935.

What Paramount lacked in financial stability, it made up in style. It was the direct antithesis of Metro-Goldwyn-Mayer. Metro, American controlled and financed, expressed a typically American impulse, endorsing the virtues of money, position and honest lust. By contrast, Paramount was European in style and approach. Its key directors and technicians were European and many of its stars came, as the filmmakers did, from Germany, where Paramount's sister company, UFA-EFA, provided a recruiting point and proving ground. Under the control of Hans Dreier, key Paramount art director, the studio's product achieved an opulence of surface never equalled by others, while its directors and stars brought to American film a sophistication and fantasy which it could not have achieved alone.

If Metro's films had polish, Paramount films had a glow. The best of them seem gilded, luminous, as rich and brocaded as Renaissance tapestry. Décor in a Paramount production was seldom, as in Metro films, merely a background; settings, draperies, gowns insinuated themselves into the action, guiding and occasionally dictating the feel of a film. Its cameramen were masters in the use of diffusers to spread the light, and in softening it to give even the simplest film a characteristic warmth. In content as well, the films exhibited this same diffusion, subtlety and style. At Paramount, the sly sexual comedy and ornate period film came into their own, the cinema approached and surpassed the stage in intellectual content. Paramount's was the cinema of half-light and suggestion; witty, intelligent, faintly corrupt.

Paramount's biggest films were in the hands of two directors totally different from each other in background, style and attitude. Cecil B. DeMille was American born, the son of a stern Episcopalian who influenced him to have a decent reverence for the Ten Commandments and the Constitution. A film-maker from the 1900s, DeMille was one of the board of directors of Paramount during the fights for power between Zukor and Lasky in 1916, and was to establish himself in time as the producer most closely embodying the essential Americanism of Thirties cinema. Ernst Lubitsch, by contrast, was completely European, born in Berlin of Jewish parents in whose clothing store he worked as a child. He became an actor on the Berlin stage, then a screen comedian and finally a director. Where DeMille's films, even the magnificent historical dramas, are obvious to the brink of cliché, Lubitsch's are sly, subtle, sometimes too much so. Lubitsch was no less capable of excess than DeMille, but the latter's films though often overblown, have an individuality not always exhibited in the work of his rival.

Despite his long association with Paramount, **CECIL B. DE-MILLE's** first sound films were made for Metro, with whom he signed a three picture contract after a fight with the Famous Players-Lasky administration. *Dynamite* (1929), his first true sound film (a previous production *The Godless Girl* (1928) had some sound added during the first days of the transition) was not typical of DeMille as modern audiences know him. A melodrama on the threadbare theme of a rich and useless socialite who marries, for legal reasons, a condemned murderer, only to have him reprieved before execution, it succeeds mainly through newcomer Charles Bickford's performance as the condemned man, Kay Johnson's spoilt heiress, and an incomparable re-creation of a mining disaster. *Madam Satan* (1930) is equally feeble as to plot — this time, Kay Johnson as a bored wife goes to a fancy-dress ball, disguised in a revealing dress as "Madam Satan", to flirt with her husband, Reginald Denny — but its finale, with the dirigible on which the party is held plunging to the ground and spilling out its passengers, gives us a sample of DeMille's talent for spectacle.

His last film for Metro, *The Squaw Man* (1931), was a remake of one he had already directed twice before, in 1914 and 1918. The thin story of an aristocrat who turns his back on society, goes out west and marries an Indian woman, it seems today ill-directed and crude. Lupe Velez as the Indian girl does little but look dejected, while Charles Bickford takes a part soon to become a sort of trademark, the ruthless murderer. Only Warner Baxter, a talented actor whose work of the Thirties is largely under-rated, convinces as the tortured exile struggling to adapt to an alien environment.

DeMille had not been happy at Metro. Control of content and casting had been for the most part out of his hands, and opportunities had not been offered for him to make the sort of films — symbolic, religious-inspired dramas — with which he had built his reputation and which he felt offered his best chance of success. The failure of an effort to form, with Frank Borzage, Lewis Milestone and King Vidor, an independent production group called The Director's Guild, depressed him still further, and in 1932 he patched up his difficulties with Paramount and returned to that studio to make one of his greatest films.

However contemptible one may find DeMille's moralising, it is impossible not to be impressed by *The Sign Of The Cross* (1932). A melodrama of sex and violence played out against ornate backgrounds, it embodies, under a veil of gimcrack Christian propaganda, a celebration of paganism. The opening scene, where Nero and his courtiers, seeming to float on a marble dais above the holocaust, look down with mingled excitement and horror at Rome burning beneath them, sets the style, to be carried on later by Fredric March's centurion who thrashes his way through the Roman crowds, driving them from his chariot wheels with a whip. As the dissolute Poppaea, Claudette Colbert easily matches Charles Laughton's simpering Nero, both of whom benefit from Mitchell Leisen's imaginative costumes.

There are few films of the Thirties more rich in sexuality than this exotic masterpiece. Poppaea bathes in a pool of asses' milk, her glistening nudity accentuated by fluffy black kittens lapping at the edge, while above them a leering gargoyle spouts milk and handmaidens sweeten it with perfumes. When a maid arrives to report some new intelligence, she is told, "Take off your clothes, come in and tell me all about it." At a later party, the Christian heroine Mercia (Elissa Landi) is mocked by the playgirl Ancaria (Joyzelle), who performs, in a brief costume, her Dance of the Naked Moon, an explicitly erotic evocation of Lesbian lust. DeMille's sadism, too, becomes apparent when a Christian boy is tortured, his agonised screams echoing up from a lighted trapdoor in the dungeon floor while his captors lounge in expectation of his surrender, or in the circus sequences, bloody slaughters summed up visually as DeMille dissolves from the face of a woman screaming excitedly to a tiger's snarling mask.

This Day And Age (1933) is a return to DeMille's late-Twenties morality plays, an unhealthy Fascist parable in which a group of boys, outraged by the way in which tycoon Charles Bickford has been able to escape a murder charge, kidnap and dangle him over a pit squirming with rats in order to elicit a confession. *Four Frightened People* (1934), also heavily symbolic, shows latent talents and weaknesses exhibiting themselves in a group of people stranded in the Malayan jungle while fleeing from an epidemic. Neither, however, is especially characteristic. DeMille's forte was the spectacular, a form to which he returned in his next film and which he was never to leave again.

Cleopatra (1934) is a sexual extravaganza in which DeMille is at his best. Claudette Colbert and a variety of Paramount contractors appear in the briefest of gowns and togas (designed by Travis Banton) to spell out a version of the Cleopatra story cobbled together from a variety of sources. The result has a fine flair and the golden surface we are used to seeing on Paramount films, effects for which Victor Milner received the year's Camera Oscar. Its opening is typical: the statue of an Egyptian god slowly turns, a nude girl lifts two smoking censers over the title, the cast list is engraved on slabs of stone. Initial shots of Cleopatra borne off protesting into the desert by charioteers are energetic, though ruined by a silly scene where they pause at some patently fake ruins near a sandhill to explain what is going on. DeMille needed the controlled lighting of the studios to bring off his best effects, and missed it in this sequence.

The Dreier sets and designs are remarkable, the Royal Barge an incredible fabrication, from its banks of oars each surmounted with a carved ram's head to the pillowed dais on which Cleopatra seduces Mark Antony (Henry Wilcoxon). At her signal, an inexhaustible supply of slave girls bursts out of every door to perform a series of dances; a garlanded ox is led in, to be caressed by semi-naked girls, one of whom just a second ahead of fade-out assumes before the animal a pose of sexual surrender; a cat-skinned group is whipped into submission by a huge slave; a net-full, clad only in sea-weed, is dredged up to sprawl out wriggling on to the deck and offer seashells full of jewels. When Antony succumbs to her wiles, Cleopatra gestures to the slaves and, as veils rise around her bed and singing girls strew them with flower petals, the cadence drummer strikes up the rhythm that sets the oars moving, and the barge moves slowly out to sea.

There are few of DeMille's films not worth considering in detail. *The Crusades* (1935) is one of the rarer and more contemplative epics, notable for Ian Keith's performance as the cultured Saladin, and some of the most striking battles ever filmed. *The Plainsman* (1937) with Gary Cooper as Wild Bill Hickok and Jean Arthur as Calamity Jane, began DeMille's series on American history, but lacked the impact of the two later films, *The Buccaneer* (1938) with Fredric March in one of his best roles as Jean Lafitte, and *Union Pacific* (1939). *The Plainsman*, however, does have one unforgettable moment; as Cooper's body lies on the ground after his murder, DeMille dissolves so that it seems to melt into the earth. Hickok has become part of the land and its mythology. This is the image of a genuine cinematic poet. DeMille was often vulgar, often false, but at his best he was a director fit to be classed with the greatest of filmic creators.

"The difference between me and Lubitsch," Erich von Stroheim once said, "is that he shows you the king on his throne and then he shows the king in his bedroom. I show the king in his bedroom first. In that way, when you see him on the throne, you've no illusions about him." This variation between von Stroheim's films and those of his great rival **ERNST LUBITSCH** accounts in the end for the ascendancy which the former has gained in modern critical circles. Lubitsch's films are witty, fast, polished, but they lack von Stroheim's bite. Even so, there are few directors of comedy who have created films of greater entertainment value or left their mark quite so indelibly on the cinema.

Lubitsch was the spirit of Paramount, embodying its European background and sophisticated style. Brought to America by Mary Pickford to direct her film *Rosita* (1923), Lubitsch joined Warner Brothers on its completion and created for them some of the period's most opulent and witty comedies. His arrival in America was part of a process which brought to Hollywood some of Germany's most talented artists. Theodore Sparkuhl, soon to become one of Paramount's top cameramen, Pola Negri and Emil Jannings, old Lubitsch stars, designers Hans Dreier and Ernst Fegté, scenarist Hans Kraly — all were eventually to enter the artistic community Lubitsch formed at Paramount and which was to re-create on American soil the old Weimar cinema.

Lubitsch's first true sound film was *The Love Parade* (1930), with Maurice Chevalier and Jeanette MacDonald. Despite the fluid camerawork and Dreier's glowing white-walled sets, Victor Schertzinger songs like "Dream Lover" and "March of the Grenadiers", the film seems trivial today, as do many of the first sound musicals. Equally unimportant are the sequences directed by Lubitsch for the omnibus film *Paramount On Parade* (1930). This extravaganza, utilising almost every Paramount player of the time, had little to recommend it.

Lubitsch directed the three songs sung by Maurice Chevalier — "The Origin Of The Apache Dance" (supposed in the film to have resulted from a fight between Chevalier and Evelyn Brent), "All I Want Is Just One Girl", with Chevalier as a gendarme taking down the names (and telephone numbers) of lovers in a Paris park, and the grand finale, "Sitting On Top Of A Rainbow And Sweeping The Clouds Away", sung by Chevalier dressed as a chimney sweep and surrounded by girls gowned and arranged as a rainbow. The latter was shot in two-colour Technicolor, as were the last reels of many early musicals, but the effect is unremarkable.

Monte Carlo (1930), a rare but disappointing Lubitsch, teamed Jeanette MacDonald with Jack Buchanan, who did not fit well into the role usually played by Chevalier. MacDonald is a countess down on her luck who goes to Monte Carlo for one last fling, accompanied by a count who poses as her hairdresser, a deception that does not dawn on her until she sees a performance of the play "Monsieur Beaucaire", and notices the obvious parallels. The film remains memorable mainly for the song "Beyond The Blue Horizon", sung by the passengers of the Blue Express to the rhythm of clattering wheels and accompanied by peasants singing in the fields around them. *The Smiling Lieutenant* (1931) is probably the rarest of all Lubitsch films. An adaptation of the Leopold Jacobson/Felix Doermann farce "The Waltz Dream", with Chevalier, Claudette Colbert and Miriam Hopkins, it was once reputed to be lost, all prints presumably destroyed by studio direction, but it is now back in general circulation.

Broken Lullaby (1932), also known as *The Man I Killed*, is one of Lubitsch's few dramas, though the film does not lack a characteristic cynicism and bite. Phillips Holmes is a young French soldier who seeks out the family of a German he killed during the war. Befriended by them, he is unable to reveal who he is, and watches with growing dismay as the dead man's father (Lionel Barrymore) begins to look on him as another son and the bereaved fiancée (Nancy Carroll) falls in love with him. The film is a measured but powerful anti-war document, full of remarkable images; Holmes playing the violin to the German family, their complex emotional attitudes clear on their faces; an acid sequence in which a tracking camera shows officers kneeling at prayer, then reverses to reveal their gleaming sabres jutting into the aisle.

One Hour With You (1932), partly directed by George Cukor, does little to improve on the earlier Chevalier/MacDonald vehicles, but *Trouble In Paradise* (1932), with remarkable performances from Miriam Hopkins, Herbert Marshall and Kay Francis, is one of the most polished comedies he was to make. The premise is wry; Marshall, an accomplished and unrepentant jewel thief, attaches himself to the rich Kay Francis, as secretary and part-time lover, and is discovered by Hopkins, another thief and also ex-girlfriend of Marshall, who applies for and gets the post of her maid. Alternately competing and philandering, the couple work independently at getting Francis's money. As a victim of Marshall's, Edward Everett Horton spends the entire film trying to remember where he has seen Francis's secretary before, his abstraction, double-takes and final triumphant recollection providing one of the film's funniest running gags. From the first shot, as the camera pans over a scene of Venice to the voice of a tenor (Caruso himself) singing "O Sole Mio", then reveals him poling a garbage gondola, the film never lets fail its pace and cynicism.

Lubitsch's episode for the omnibus film *If I Had A Million* (1932) was unremarkable — Charles Laughton, as a humble clerk given a million dollars, walks up innumerable flights of stairs to give his boss a rousing raspberry and resign — but *Design For Living* (1933) his adaptation of Noël Coward's play with Fredric March, Miriam Hopkins and Gary Cooper in the parts originally played by Alfred Lunt, Lynn Fontanne and Coward himself, was accomplished, despite miscasting of Cooper in the Coward role. As the girl who moves in with the penurious team of artist and playwright and switches with casual promiscuity from one to the other, Miriam Hopkins is delightful. Ben Hecht boasts that he deleted all but one of Coward's lines from the script — the toast "For the good of our immortal souls" — but, even if this is so, the Coward spirit remains; Hopkins concluding a long "cool-off" speech to Cooper with a referral to the three friends' "gentlemen's agreement" about sex, and then throwing herself down on the couch with the comment "But I'm no gentleman"; the three standing around in their denuded apartment sharing a meagre meal of one frankfurter, Hopkins conversationally requesting March to "Pass the mustard".

Of all Lubitsch's operetta adaptations, *The Merry Widow* (1934) is the best. The film was made for Metro, but has all the Paramount polish, despite the problems Lubitsch had in getting Cedric Gibbons to fall in with his extravagant demands in the matter of sets. People criticised Metro for allowing Lubitsch to change a frothy romance into a satire on the ludicrousness of sex, but the combination of disenchanted dialogue and the lush Lehar music (with lyrics by Rodgers, Hart and Kahn) gives this film a formal tension lacking in his earlier efforts. Chevalier plays the rake Danilo with style and charm, while MacDonald as the widow is at the height of her opulent pre-Raphaelite beauty. Her songs, especially "Velia", shot by the brilliant Oliver Marsh from a low angle, showing her spotted high on a balcony while in the foreground gipsy musicians play in half silhouette, are imaginatively directed, and her appearance in the film is, on balance, probably the peak of her career.

As in all Lubitsch's films, supporting performances enlarge the impact of *The Merry Widow*. George Barbier as the cuckolded King Achmed, Una Merkel as his wife, Edward Everett Horton as the hapless ambassador — all outstrip the principals. There are some typical Lubitsch sight gags, as well as many from the script — the king returning unexpectedly to the queen's bedroom, entering briefly, walking out and down the corridor trying abstractedly to buckle on a sword belt far too short for him, stopping, understanding, then racing back to find Chevalier hiding there; a conversation with adviser Donald Meek, who reveals that there is unrest in the kingdom: the shepherds are talking. The king is worried. "Influential shepherds?" Meek shrugs. "East side shepherds". "Intellectuals!" the king says contemptuously, "Let them talk". And Horton, ambassador to Paris, receiving a letter in code, the first word, "Darling", being translatable according to his code book as "Of all the idiots in the diplomatic service, you are the worst".

In 1935, Lubitsch became production manager of Paramount and relinquished briefly his directorial duties. During this period he received a credit on *Desire* (1936), directed by Frank Borzage but "Produced under the personal supervision of Ernst Lubitsch". After an unhappy year as an executive, he resigned to return to directing, and did *Angel* (1937) with Dietrich, and *Bluebeard's Eighth Wife* (1938), with Claudette Colbert and Gary Cooper. Neither was especially successful, and the latter marked the end of Lubitsch's association with Paramount. His next two films were for Metro, including his last Thirties film and probably the last great comedy of the decade.

Ninotchka (1939) is a film not especially typical of anybody associated with it. Garbo plays comedy with more enthusiasm than skill, Lubitsch directs a story that is unusually free of sexual innuendo and marked more by the wit of scenarists Billy Wilder and Charles Brackett than his own. The "Lubitsch style" in which much was made of subtleties — glances, finger movements, raised eyebrows — has disappeared. Instead we have a hard, brightly lit, cynical comedy with the wise-crack completely in control. In a grotesque self-parody, Garbo mocks her own image, impersonating with no particular relish a Communist commissar, clumsy and gauche, who falls for a Parisian *flaneur*. Sig Rumann, Felix Bressart and Alexander Granach play three Russian émigrés in love with high life and fearful of having it denied them, an emotion with which they, as European immigrant actors, would have been familiar. Like so much Forties comedy, *Ninotchka* is flip and funny, but one seldom avoids the feeling that it is the audience rather than the situation that is being mocked.

Ernst Lubitsch, in retrospect, seems a director who never adequately adjusted to the necessities of the American cinema. His style and approach were those of Germany, and without the sophistication of European audiences he found himself forced increasingly to talk down to his public. As the Thirties wore on and audience ability to appreciate the best in cinema was eroded by cheap publicity and the assault of the mass media, his work became cruder, exhibiting the very vulgarity which some people erroneously found in his earlier films. Lubitsch's great films came in the time of balance, when American and European influences were equalised. His European-influenced films are decadent, his American-influenced films crude, but those of the years 1931-1934 are as great as any the cinema has produced.

Lubitsch has been classed by some as a technical innovator, but aside from his perfection of the visual gag, achieved usually by a slow pan or track across the action to point up an amusing relationship, his contribution to technique was limited. The much-praised skill in camera movement was seldom more assured than that of his contemporaries, while the reliance on visual puns seems less the action of a pioneer than of somebody not entirely at ease in sound cinema. His use of sound was occasionally brilliant, but more often he made up with music and photographic glitter the deficiencies caused by an imperfect understanding of the medium. If we should consider any Paramount director an innovator it must be the erratic, mannered, but generally ingenious **ROUBEN MAMOULIAN**.

For sheer technical competence in the film-making process, Mamoulian can have few equals. His films abound in visual and aural tricks, exotic effects, juxtapositions of sound, image and music that verge occasionally on the ridiculous but seldom slip over. A Russian-born stage director famous for his New York première presentation of the play *Porgy* (by Dorothy and DuBose Hayward), he brought to all his films the heightened sensitivity to décor and lighting that marks the great theatrical creators. His first film, *Applause* (1929), was, however, a coldly realistic work owing little to the flamboyance of the stage. As an ageing burlesque queen driven to suicide by degradation and finally by her daughter's determination to become a strip-teaser and begin on the same road, Helen Morgan gives one of her best screen performances. Mamoulian's use of moving camera is impressive in a few cases, notably that in which Morgan is recalling her past. The camera lingers on her face, then pans slowly to a picture of her as a young girl, then back to her again. The point is made with economy and quiet pathos.

It is in its evocation of burlesque's down-at-heel atmosphere that

Applause succeeds best. From the opening, with a line of ageing blowsy chorines performing with scant sexuality for equally ageing but randy patrons, Mamoulian seems determined to give us as true a picture as is possible of this grubby world. Although only in her thirties, Helen Morgan brilliantly suggests the dissipation and maudlin sickness of a fiftyish alcoholic. Her suicide, with the bathroom mirror mocking her by reflecting a face as chalky and lifeless as that of a clown, and the montage of neon lights and scenes of revelry which accompanies her death, make no concessions to sentiment, although Mamoulian is not above lyricism when showing the happiness of the young lovers, tracking deliriously across the New York skyline (*sans* Empire State Building) or through the seething crowds of Penn Station to catch the couple at the peak of a stunning crane shot to which he adds the visual exclamation mark of a startled flock of pigeons. In its combination of melodrama and realism, of style and sentiment, *Applause* is one of the major films of this or any other period.

Mamoulian's next film, *City Streets* (1931), was his first in Hollywood — *Applause* had been made in Paramount's New York studios — and in content and approach differed considerably. Based on an idea by Dashiell Hammett, it was a conventional gangster drama, this time employing the talents of Gary Cooper and Sylvia Sidney. Originally a vehicle designed to revive the failing career of Paramount's biggest silent star, Clara Bow, which had slumped alarmingly at the coming of sound, it was based on an early Bow success, *Ladies Of The Mob*. Before she had been fully prepared by Mamoulian for the role, however, Bow had a collapse, and the part, after having been declined by Nancy Carroll, went at Mamoulian's suggestion to Sylvia Sidney. Skilful location shooting, visual and aural symbolism, tracking shots and artfully lit sequences abound, and there is an early use of overlapping dialogue in a scene where Sidney in jail relives conversations out of her past, the words garbled and confused by her terror; but the overall effect of *City Streets* is more confusing than impressive.

Doctor Jekyll And Mister Hyde (1932) was the third attempt made by Hollywood to adapt Stevenson's novel, and the most successful. The penchant for melodramatic effects which had occasionally marred

Mamoulian's earlier work was completely appropriate to the fantastic and bizarre, and it is significant that, after this film, he never returned to the field of social realism from which his first two films had drawn their subjects. The world of weird transformations and mental distress is one in which he is completely at home, and the assurance of his work in this case is marked. Mamoulian's inventions for the scenes showing Fredric March's change from Jekyll to Hyde would alone have made this film memorable. Determined to engineer the transformations without resorting to cuts or opticals, Mamoulian conceived on the spur of the moment a system in which specially toned make-up, coloured lights and coloured filters were used to change the look of March's face. By personally manipulating a hastily constructed system of filters in front of the camera and employing red and green light, first to obscure then reveal portions of make-up, Mamoulian was able to achieve effects still unequalled today. The soundtrack, similarly complex, uses portions of Bach as well as eerier tonalities fabricated from the sound of a gong played backwards, painting on the track and a distorted recording of Mamoulian's own heart. While some criticism is possible of the performances and script, as a work of cinematic imagination this film is difficult to fault.

Love Me Tonight (1932) is Mamoulian's first venture away from screen drama and into the world of humorous fantasy that he was to inhabit for years. Gay, charming, witty, it is everything that the Lubitsch musicals should have been but never were. Chevalier and MacDonald are impossibly good — one doubted that such performances were in them. The music is superb, but Mamoulian improves it with imaginative handling. Scored and planned like an opera, *Love Me Tonight* sweeps us along on its songs. "Isn't It Romantic" is sung first in Paris, picked up by people in the streets, then by passengers on a train, until finally a troop of marching soldiers carries it to MacDonald dreaming at the window of her chateau. Later she is to sing "Lover" as her horse and carriage whirl her through the forest, a breathless delivery aurally echoing the scene's visual pace.

It is no wonder that the studio heads were terrified by Mamoulian's bravura style in this film. Even by modern standards, the slow motion retreat of the huntsmen and their horses from the cottage where they have discovered the lovers is advanced, as are the half-mocking low key lighting and sprawling shadows of Chevalier's "I'm An Apache" song. The opening sequence, with the sounds of a waking Paris blended skilfully into a complex musical rhythm, is copied direct from Mamoulian's stage production of *Porgy And Bess*, but it is still surprising today, while one never quite gets used to the three old aunts who appear occasionally like baroque witches to mutter in rhymed couplets of MacDonald's prospects or, on one occasion, to bark like dogs in astonishment. If there is a better musical of the Thirties, one wonders what it can be. One had to wait until the Sixties delights of Jacques Demy to find anything comparable.

Mamoulian's next three works are not especially striking, though none lacks eccentricity. *Queen Christina* (1933), made on invitation at M-G-M, is still one of Garbo's more interesting films, due largely to Mamoulian's refusal to be overawed by the great star. To him, she was "a wonderful instrument", and nothing more. He uses her cynically, creating a performance not through inspiration but by manipulation. The sequence in which Christina moves around the room where she has been happy, caressing the objects in it and saying goodbye to her happiness as well as to them; the final enigmatic close-up as she stands in the prow of the boat carrying the body of her lover back to Spain; both were created almost completely by Mamoulian. In the first, he had her move in time to a metronome, imposing a musical formality on her actions, while the second was achieved by directing that she clear her mind completely and think of nothing, Daniels's inexorable movement of the camera into close-up forcing the audience to read into the silent face their own confused emotions.

John Gilbert is not especially good as the male lead, but works competently in a difficult part. A story to the effect that Gilbert got the role on Garbo's orders in preference to an inexperienced Laurence Olivier now seems apocryphal. Mamoulian claims that his test of Olivier showed him to be totally unsuitable.

Song Of Songs (1933) gave Mamoulian the use of another "wonderful instrument", Marlene Dietrich, but it is typical of the man that he was

46

not influenced by her legendary von Sternberg aura and used brutally high key lighting that stripped the gloss from her as it built it up on Garbo. The story, in which Dietrich played a country girl enamoured of sculptor Brian Aherne, did nothing for her, though when the latter, after carving her in the nude, hands her over to a decaying aristocrat, she has the opportunity to reverse her tremulous and virginal image to that of a cool, vengeful *grande dame*. The film comes to life only briefly, as when Aherne, watching Dietrich's silhouette as she strips to pose for him, caresses the statue he has made of her, or the nobleman's discarded mistress and rapacious secretary prowl in the garden on his wedding night watching the couple silhouetted in the lighted window above. The rest, unfortunately, is inferior to Mamoulian's best work. This may be due to the fact that Mamoulian was caught in a Paramount/von Sternberg dispute, taking over as the latter's nominee while von Sternberg went secretly to Germany in the hope of setting up independent production there with Dietrich.

We Live Again (1934) made for independent producer Sam Goldwyn, was a meagre adaptation of Tolstoy's "Resurrection", notable only for some variable Gregg Toland camerawork and the décor of Broadway stage designer Serge Soudeikin whom Mamoulian brought especially to Hollywood for the film. Mamoulian was a last-minute replacement for Lowell Sherman, who died during preproduction, for *Becky Sharp* (1935). He also used a New York designer for this film, and Robert Edmond Jones was to make a major contribution to its success. *Becky Sharp* was the first film made in the new three-colour Technicolor. There had been colour films of various kinds since the days of Lumière, but most of them had depended on filters or some form of tinting for their effects. Two-colour Technicolor departed from this practice in that it involved two negatives, exposed in the same camera at the same time, but differing in that each was shot through a coloured filter so as to record separate parts of the spectrum. In the laboratory, the two negatives were dyed in the basic colours of pink/orange and blue/green (cyan), and the two emulsion layers placed on one projection print by a process similar to letterpress printing. The result, with its bilious skies and shrimp pink complexions modulating to brick red, was more surprising than beautiful, and doomed, as everybody knew, to eventual extinction.

Three-colour Technicolor was an advance on this system only in that three separate negatives were now run through the camera, then dyed yellow, magenta and cyan. Although bulky cameras and the problems of processing posed difficulties, the system did make it possible for the first time to show shades of colour with some accuracy, and therefore to use colour dramatically. Mamoulian jumped at the opportunity to indulge his penchant for the bizarre, especially when he was given as his subject Thackeray's *Vanity Fair* with its Napoleonic setting and dramatic action. There are some well-organised effects; red and white cannon flashes against an evening sky; a scarlet cloak lying discarded on a white marble staircase; and perhaps the most remarkable sequence in the film, a military ball which, at the news of Waterloo, slowly drains of every colour except the red of military uniforms. Mamoulian admits that, logically, this is ridiculous — the soldiers would have been the first to leave — but, as in all his films, logic has never been in any way comparable to artistic effect.

The remainder of Rouben Mamoulian's Thirties' films were undistinguished. *The Gay Desperado* (1936) was a confused mixture of singing bandits and low comedy, while *High, Wide And Handsome* (1937) offered little except a few agreeable songs by Irene Dunne, including the pretty "Folks That Live On The Hill", and some half-hearted attempts to evoke the drama of the early oilstrikes in Pennsylvania and the efforts of oil-men to get their product to market. Only the ending is in the Mamoulian tradition. Beset by rival railroadmen, the oil pipeline builders are rescued in the nick of time by a circus which comes thundering over the hill, elephants and all, to pitch into the fight. Acrobats swing head down over the crowd wielding Indian clubs, elephants pick up men and fling them into the river, the strong man lays about him with vigour. *Golden Boy* (1939), from the Clifford Odets play about a boxing violin player is no better than the two films preceding it, and provides a disappointing end to an erratic but often brilliant Thirties career. Mamoulian tried to make cinema

Marlene Dietrich, Lionel Atwill and the marriage bed of Rouben Mamoulian's THE SONG OF SONGS (above). Maurice Chevalier as the rake Danilo and Jeanette MacDonald at the height of her opulent pre-Raphaelite beauty in Ernst Lubitsch's THE MERRY WIDOW (below left). Michael Curtiz, "inescapably one of the best directors to emerge in the cinema", seated to right of camera watching Errol Flynn, Donald Crisp and David Niven on the set of THE CHARGE OF THE LIGHT BRIGADE (below right).

*Errol Flynn as
Peter Blood in
Michael Curtiz'
CAPTAIN BLO*

*Director Mervyn
LeRoy is seated
left. The players
Wallace Beery a
Marie Dressler,
stars of TUGBO
ANNIE, one of
LeRoy's earlier
pictures.*

into music, just as Lubitsch tried to make it conversation and von Sternberg painting. All failed, Mamoulian perhaps worst of all, because his goal was the most impossible of attainment. His films remain, however, fascinating signposts along one of the more interesting cinematic dead-ends.

Of the regular contract directors at Paramount, none rose to the level of those employed at Metro, nor were calculating enough to descend to the tough, cynical story-telling style of Warners, though both Mitchell Leisen and Josef von Sternberg created films individual enough to be considered separately, in Chapters 6 and 9 respectively. Of the rest, Wesley Ruggles, despite the reputation of *Cimarron* (1930), is not a director of note; his comedies are limp, his style among the most flaccid in the cinema. Alexander Hall worked hard to breathe life into his routine comedies but seldom succeeded. Robert Florey brought to his work, especially the Akim Tamiroff vehicles *King Of Gamblers* (1937) and *Dangerous To Know* (1938), a continental polish and characteristic Paramount gloss, but he lacked the wit of Leisen or the visual imagination of von Sternberg that might have made them memorable. (For a consideration of his fantasy film *Murders In The Rue Morgue* and *The Florentine Dagger* see Chapter 5.)

Paramount was among the most interesting phenomena of the Thirties. Its interior politics were complex, its artistic output variable but of a high average quality. Loose ends abound. One would like the time to investigate more deeply the significance of the German-American axis of Paramount finance, the degree to which UFA-EFA was affected by its American sister company, and vice versa. The Eisenstein debacle, F. W. Murnau's work with Paramount and that of Paul Leni; all these deserve deeper examination than is possible here. Reluctantly, one must conclude on the perhaps over-simplified summary that Paramount was a studio of contrasts. It had, in von Sternberg, one of the greatest directors of all time, and, in Mitchell Leisen, one of the most underrated. It had the most prodigal, DeMille, and the most decadent, Lubitsch. Yet, with all this, it never achieved the greatness of Metro. The reasons, if they could ever be isolated, would make fascinating reading.

4: The Studios: Warners

METRO MADE films for the middle class, full of noble socialites and madcap stunt pilots who always settled down in the end, and Paramount for the upper class, supplying a combination of sophisticated dialogue and baroque setting that was *très snob*. At Warner Brothers, however, films were made for and about the working class. Their musicals, born of the depression, combined stories of hard-working chorus girls and ambitious young tenors with opulent production numbers, both designed to appeal directly to the patrons in the stalls, as did the dramas of taxi-drivers, bell-hops and dance hall girls struggling to make ends meet in the brawl of New York. Lighting was low-key, to heighten atmosphere and make the best of cheap sets. Elegance at Warners reached its peak with Warren William in a double-breaster and snap brim hat eating lobster on the Embarcadero, yet even so feeble an apex as this was a concession from a studio where gloss and polish were considered useless affectation.

Warners was founded by two men who could hardly have been expected to set much store by elegance. Harry B. and Jack Warner had been butchers before they got into films, but their business acumen served them as well in movies as it had elsewhere. Though they formed their company well into the 1920s, they had soon bought themselves both a production and a distribution operation. The first was acquired when the Associated Producers group — independents like Dwan, Vidor, Sennett and Maurice Tourneur — sold out in 1921 to First National Pictures, who later amalgamated, as had the Vitagraph Company in 1925, with Warners. In 1929, Warners' films were still endorsed with odd combinations of the Vitagraph, Warners and First National brand marks, but by the early Thirties "Warner Brothers" was becoming known as a title, and it never faded after that.

Paramount's financial difficulties were minor compared with those of Warners, which suffered heavily in a battle with Zukor for a more substantial exhibition circuit. By the late 1920s, Warners was in severe straits. Cutting corners became an art. Stars were contracted at low salaries and held to their contracts until the most had been wrung from them. Directors worked at an incredible rate, producing as many as five features a year. The basic film at Warners was the seven reel programme picture, a melodrama, usually about criminals or some form of low life, which ran for seventy minutes and never let go for one moment of the audience's attention. It is no coincidence that Ralph Dawson, Warners' top editor, won three Oscars in the Thirties for his work. Pace was more than Warners' trademark—it was a necessity.

This was the cinema of poverty. Bette Davis remarked bitterly, "We had the answer, the successor or the sequel to everything." Under executive head Hal Wallis, notorious for his parsimony, the studio extracted the last drop of worth from every production and star. Despite this, Warners during the late Twenties steadily lost money, outpunched by its larger rivals, Paramount and Metro. It was a desperate company that, casting around for some gimmick to boost sales, hit on the idea of putting more money and work into the then primitive sound cinema concept. The successful première in 1926 of *Don Juan*, with its synchronised sound effects and music, not to mention a film introduction spoken by Will Hays, chairman of the production code authority, encouraged Warners to produce *The Better 'Ole* and *When A Man Loves* (1926), both with synchronised music, plus a number of short films featuring famous singers. In 1927, it released the most historic sound film of all, and the first to feature synchronised music, effects and dialogue in the same production, Alan Crosland's *The Jazz Singer*. While other companies dithered, sound films caught on and made Warners rich.

By 1929, Warners was among the most active of the studios, financially stable for the first time in its complex history. The old habits, however, remained, and were in fact reinforced by the competition following the perfection of sound equipment, when rival companies, having paid ruinous prices for patents on sound systems other than those owned by Warners, set out cold-bloodedly to win back their money at Warners' expense. For the most part they failed. Warners' films were the most perfectly economical exercises in cinema mechanics of which Hollywood was capable. There was no fat on them, either as art or entertainment. (Producer Louis Edelman speaks of cutting single frames from every shot in a film to speed up its pace.) The Warners' team — set designers Anton Grot and Carl Jules Weyl, couturier John "Orry" Kelly, cameramen Gaetano Gaudio, Barney McGill, Sol Polito — was a competent one, but as a film-making tool it functioned best in the hands of two great directors, Mervyn LeRoy and Michael Curtiz.

Inescapably one of the best directors ever to emerge in the cinema, **MICHAEL CURTIZ** lays a substantial claim to being the greatest director of the Thirties. Like Van Dyke, however, Curtiz was a victim of the studio system. The talent that might have produced masterpieces if left to mature in peace was cast and hardened by Warners' ruthless insistence on pace and production. But, unlike Van Dyke, Curtiz did not turn into a mere motion picture machine. His films have a ferocity about them which suggests he refused to allow the material he was given to dominate him. No one was more adept at forcing the pace of films, at hammering even the most intransigent star into submission. Hated by actors, remembered mainly for his heavily accented and mispronounced English, Curtiz seems the embodiment of a European tradition totally opposed to the elegance and sly wit of Lubitsch and his Paramount associates. Curtiz's Germany is that of the Reeperbahn, the brothels of Berlin, the slums of Munich and Hamburg. It is not to be wondered at that his films are among the most pitiless, grotesque and erotic in the history of the cinema.

From 1930 to 1939, Curtiz made the incredible total of forty-four films, few of which survive. Among the earliest of his masterpieces is *The Strange Love of Molly Louvain* (1932), a ruthless and cynical picture of low life with Lee Tracy as a disenchanted newspaperman. The milieu of slum streets and hotel rooms is re-created with chilling detail, the story told with a pitiless intensity. *Doctor X* (1932) is one of the greatest of the classic horror films, incorporating most of the key Germanic elements; necrophilia, dismemberment, rape. Preston

Foster, laboratory assistant to the clubfooted Doctor X (Lionel Atwill) smears himself at night with a grisly paste of "synthetic flesh", draws on gnarled gloves of a similar material, and moves through the empty streets to strangle, his shadow with its swollen bestial profile sliding across moonlit walls. There are terrifying sequences: a skeleton stirring as the life-giving essence of synthetic flesh evaporates from an overturned bottle, Foster's grotesque metamorphosis from man into monster as he smears the obscene surrogate over his face. But none equals the finale, where Lee Tracy's reporter is flung about like a doll as he battles the monster in a Caligari-esque corridor, a more effective evocation of superhuman strength than even the great James Whale could engineer.

Cabin in the Cotton (1932) was one of Richard Barthelmess's last big films, but one of the first to show off the talents of young Warners contract player Bette Davis. The story of class conflict on a Southern plantation is enlivened only by her playing as the rich girl who seduces Barthelmess, the son of a sharecropper educated by the local landowner to become his heir. The blending of sound and image in the scene where, stripping in view of the panting young man, she sings "Willie the Weeper" in a breathy southern contralto and undoes with an electric rustle the bow of her dress, makes it one of the great voyeuristic experiences the cinema has afforded us. This film, effective, but inappropriate by virtue of its rural location to Curtiz's style, is not as satisfactory as the one which follows it, *20,000 Years In Sing Sing* (1933). As the girl of jailed mobster Spencer Tracy, Davis is superb; tough, laconic, but essentially vulnerable. The prison background suits Curtiz, and he obviously found agreeably unromantic the ending where Tracy, confessing to a murder committed by Davis, goes in the final scenes to death in the electric chair.

Series thrillers were a Warners speciality and, like all studios, they owned their stable of characters, including Perry Mason and S. S. Van Dine's patrician sleuth Philo Vance. William Powell's performance as Vance in *The Kennel Murder Case* (1933) is sometimes alarmingly vague, but Curtiz brings to the unremarkable story of a murdered collector of *chinoiserie* his usual callous skill. Few films of the Thirties are as perfect examples of technique in the service of the cinema. Curtiz's use of the wipe in *The Kennel Murder Case* is superb. The fingerprinting of six suspects is shown with a shot of the first bending over the pad, then five consecutive portraits of the others, each wiped briskly away by the next. The guard on a train says, "Send a wire to the police and say — " cut to Eugene Pallette's police officer reading the contents of the telegram to a subordinate. Split screen, zip pans, moving camera — all combine to force the narrative pace relentlessly. Curtiz, where it is appropriate, breaks every rule. The wind-up explanation of the locked room murder, a silly business of pins, thread and keyholes, is shot like a science demonstration, unmysterious and satisfyingly clear. Hard to believe that the same director a few reels before does an interview without showing faces at all, lingering instead on the impassive visages of Chinese figurines staring down, a disturbing, imaginative scene.

Mandalay (1934), a steamy tropical melodrama, was made to measure for its stars. Kay Francis played her speciality, the weary woman of the world, wounded by fate, Ricardo Cortez a charming cad. Only Curtiz's style gives the film any hold on immortality. Francis's matronly good looks are shown off well, in a scene where she lolls on Cortez's yacht, her face shaded by a parasol, and later startling appearance sheathed in silver at a notorious brothel and bar. "They call her 'Spot White' ", an awed patron remarks. "It should be 'Spot Cash' ", his companion says morosely. Wipes and opticals generally are used to good effect, and Curtiz derives particular pleasure from the grotesque climax, imparting a Grand Guignol relish to the scene where Francis poisons her inconvenient lover and dumps him out the porthole of a riverboat.

Kay Francis also appears, with Leslie Howard, in the eccentric *British Agent* (1934), playing Lenin's stenographer in an unusual melodrama of revolutionary Russia. Howard as one of a group of foreign diplomats hiding in Moscow during the revolution is somewhat out of touch with the part, but the supporting roles — J. Carrol Naish as Trotsky, Irving Pichel as Stalin — are well done. Curtiz again gives us remarkable sequences; an ambassadorial ball interrupted by a stream of machine gun bullets ripping across the mirrors that line the salon, soldiers raging through the streets in decrepit army trucks, and an odd vignette concerning one of the diplomats who goes out to contact a Russian army officer. Curtiz cuts promptly to the two men walking through a gate as part of a group. The diplomat, smoking nervously, says with a grin, "Well, Colonel, at least I found you". The next shot shows them lined up against a wall with the others and executed.

The same brutal cynicism turns up in *The Case Of The Curious Bride* (1935), with Warren William, Warners' "answer" to John Barrymore, well cast as Perry Mason. "Have you ever wanted to strangle your wife?", a tugboat captain asks his mate in the second shot, continuing that, if he did, Perry Mason could get him off. There is a cut from the paper the captain is holding to the same edition in the hands of a newsboy, who walks along the crowded fishmarkets of the Embarcadero of San Francisco to sell one to William, busy choosing a lobster for lunch. Ten minutes later, we have a mystery, artfully unfolded by Curtiz with appropriate cynicism. A lunch with the coroner is adjourned to the morgue where, over their coffee, William and friends sit in on an autopsy. The coffin turns out, however, to hold nothing but a wooden Indian. Visiting his client in jail, William serves her a sumptuous dinner in the visitor's room, complete with candelabra and silver chafing-dish, then considerately visits an old friend in the death cell to give him a last meal he has dreamed about — snails. Curtiz's fascination with new transition devices shows up in an unusual combined out-of-focus shot and cut. Most of the film's scenes are bridged in this way; but one remembers best the weird gastronomical motif.

After 1935, both Warners and Curtiz began to undergo a change. The studio's films became less frantic, tending to spread themselves occasionally in spectacular dramas and period pictures as the public came to accept Warners as a major studio. Curtiz's *Captain Blood* (1935), while not especially extravagant by today's standards nor indeed by those of the time, is a polished period adventure film, shot with a richness not typical of Warners but soon to become so. The harsh lighting had softened, giving many interiors a gentle, almost Paramount glow. Early sequences of captives held by the Spaniards in the East Indies make much of fretted light in the von Sternberg tradition and the sheen of skin in shadow, though the slaves' escape and their formation into a pirate gang under the leadership of Peter Blood (Errol Flynn) is done with the old Curtiz panache. This film was a turning point for him. Highly respected by Jack Warner as a craftsman, he was placed in charge of further vehicles for Errol Flynn, then being built up by Warners as an "answer" to Clark Gable. Curtiz's Flynn films — *Charge of the Light Brigade* (1936), *The Perfect Specimen* (1937), *The Adventures of Robin Hood* (1938), *Dodge City* (1939) among them — made him a top name at Warners, and their romanticism softened his style in a way that would make him capable of directing his great Forties films—*Casablanca, The Santa Fe Trail, Mildred Pierce*. (Credit for much of Warners' success with the Errol Flynn adventures belongs to second-unit director B. Reeves "Breezy" Eason, who managed the action sequences in most of them.)

Kid Galahad (1937) is one of the last Curtiz films to exhibit the old energy, taking a final, almost affectionate look at the grubby scene of his early triumphs. His picture of professional boxing's ruthlessness is however mellowed by a warmer attitude to character. Edward G. Robinson's tough trainer/manager is well played, exhibiting some of the Levantine elegance which made him so memorable in Howard Hawks's *Barbary Coast*. Scenes at a party where, having lost most of his money, Robinson blows the rest on a spree for friends and his mistress Fluff (Bette Davis), are gay to just the right hysterical degree. The camera tracks over dishevelled girls and disarranged furniture to discover Robinson having a haircut and Davis busily serving drinks with indefatigable charm. "I gave you a haircut three days ago and you were having a party then," the barber observes. Robinson smiles grimly. "Same party," he says.

The plot, involving a bellhop (Wayne Morris) whom Robinson trains to world champion, is poorly achieved, perhaps because Curtiz insists on examining the romance that grows up between him and Fluff, and the complications that ensue when Morris falls for Robinson's sister (Jane Bryan). Robinson's incestuous jealousy, reminiscent of Paul Muni's in Hawks's *Scarface*, is adequately conveyed, but the tensions engendered detract from the impact of the central theme, Morris's climb to fame as a boxer. The fights, however, are superbly done. After a typically cynical beginning, with Curtiz cutting from an important fight to an argument in the audience so that we miss the vital knockout, he gives us some of the most violent battles ever seen on film. Morris is literally flung across the ring by punches, reeling from corner to corner totally out of control; knockouts are hammer blows, sending men crashing to the canvas like felled trees. If only for these sequences, *Kid Galahad* is worth seeing.

Curtiz is fitfully on form in *The Adventures of Robin Hood* (1938), which he completed after William Keighley had been taken off the project at Jack Warner's direction, Keighley's limp style seeming to him to be inappropriate to the theme. The final sword duel between Flynn and Basil Rathbone is a triumph of Curtiz's direction and Carl Jules Weyl's castle sets (Academy Award 1938) but much of the rest is marred by confusion of intent and Flynn's indifferent acting. Of Curtiz's last films of the period, only *Daughters Courageous* (1939) seems worth remembering. A gentle family drama acted with dignity and charm it is one of the most pleasant of its kind. James Wong Howe's photography of the Monterey locations is soft and flattering to the actors, setting for Fay Bainter and Claude Rains the pattern they were to follow later in their Forties' careers.

The idea, of a close-knit family of mother and four grown-up daughters disrupted first by the mother's impending re-marriage then the reappearance after twenty years of her ex-husband (Claude Rains), could have been a wallow of sentiment, but Curtiz observes his characters with skill. Rains's wry humour, his half-concealed contempt for the settled bachelor his wife is to marry (Donald Crisp), the cunning with which he wins over his daughters, all exhibit a complete co-operation between director and star. John Garfield as the layabout who wants to marry the youngest daughter (Priscilla Lane) turns in one of his best socialist-oriented performances, assailing every institution in sight. "Buy me a beer?" he asks Lane. "Are you serious?" "I'm *thirsty*." Confronted in court by allegations that the piece of Moby Dick's tooth he has been trying to peddle to tourists is obviously a fraud because Moby Dick was invented by a writer, he retorts, "Well, I can only say that he made him seem very real to *me*." The ending, with the rejection of both Rains and Garfield by the warm family circle into which they had tried to insinuate themselves, is tough, though enlivened, as is the entire film, with humour and charm. For its intelligent use of small town locations, its skilled acting, fine camerawork and evenly paced, sympathetic direction, it surpasses everything of its type.

Less cold a thinker than Curtiz, not so competent a technician but probably, on balance, more deserving of praise as an artist of ideas, **MERVYN LEROY** made for Warners some of its most polished and ambitious productions during the Thirties. If, however, the poorer Curtiz films are disappointing, LeRoy's failures are impossible to watch. When his initial concept was faulty or failed through heavy-handed scripting he could be as banal as Henry King at his worst. It needed a firm central theme to sustain LeRoy, a solid anchor for his speculation, and it was when he had this that his films reached heights at least as lofty as those scaled by Curtiz. But given a silly plot, he had no concept of changing it as Curtiz did. He merely gave up and let it control his film.

LeRoy's Thirties' reputation rests today on two films, *They Won't Forget* (1939) and the Edward G. Robinson's vehicle *Little Caesar* (1931). Adapted from W. R. Burnett's morally indignant novel, the latter competes with a number of other attacks on organised crime — *The Secret Six*, *Scarface* foremost among them — but fails to produce any major variations on the theme. As in most films of this kind, material which begins as criticism modulates slowly into grudging admiration. Robinson's callous, stupid Rico is initially objectionable, but his rise to power over the corpses of his enemies is accompanied by a modulation in tone until we find ourselves distressed by his death in a back alley, moved by his final bemused words, "Mother of Mercy, is this the end of Rico?" As in all Warners' films of the time, lighting and sets aptly convey the grubbiness of the background, but despite LeRoy's admiration for the film and the meticulous way he researched its settings, it is only when *Little Caesar* is taken out of context that it appears as a masterpiece. Placed among the Warners' crime dramas, it becomes merely one of a dozen equally capable exercises in the genre.

Less typical is *I Am A Fugitive From A Chain Gang* (1932), originally intended as a ganster melodrama to cash in on Warners' newest star, Paul Muni, still famous for his role in Hawks's *Scarface*, but transmuted by LeRoy into a ruthless attack on social injustice. Muni as the man wrongly accused of a theft, tried, jailed, tortured, finally condemned to a life of flight as a fugitive, achieves one of his best performances but, as in so many others of the period, background and lighting give the film its oppressive atmosphere. The crowded verminous huts where the convicts are kept, the thick shadows which seem to clog the air: both add to the impact of LeRoy's realistic direction. The flogging scenes are especially sickening, evoking with vicious power the brutality and agony of the whip. Nor has any director managed to end his film on so cold a note as does LeRoy, with the hissed exchange between Muni and his sweetheart after he has crept to her house at night for food: "But how do you get along; how do you live?" and the whispered reply, "I steal."

Two Seconds (1932), one of the more unusual Warners' low-life dramas, provided LeRoy once again with a story strongly biased towards social comment. The premise is disturbing. A group of reporters gathered to watch an electrocution talks about the mechanics of death. A student gathering material for a term paper asks, "How long does it take for him to die?" "Between when the current hits him and his heart stops, about two seconds." "I bet those two seconds will be the longest of his life," the student remarks. Then the prisoner is brought in. It is Edward G. Robinson, convicted wife murderer. Contemptuously he looks over the audience, sits down . . . the switch is pulled—and he remembers it all: his first visit to a dance hall where he meets the girl he is to marry (Vivienne Os-

59

borne); the terrifying accident in which his best friend (Preston Foster) is killed, falling in a spinning, screaming descent from the building on which both work; his swift mental collapse at the death of Foster, his wife's whining complaints about lack of money; the crazy moment when he kills her, and the half remembered trial at the end of which he is sent raving insanely to the death cell.

Vicious and disenchanted, *Two Seconds* is unrelieved in its black mood. The homely Robinson retreats from a blind date with an even more lumpy woman to find himself in a ten cent dance hall, confronted by a line of weary, gum-chewing hostesses who view without surprise the mis-shapen clientele waiting to paw them. His eventual marriage to one such girl is a grotesque farce. Encouraged by his fiancée to drink himself silly on speakeasy gin, he is dragged to the justice of the peace, still with the teacup out of which the liquor was served stuck on his finger. Everything in the film contributes to the truth of Robinson's musings, encouraged by the view from the top of the buildings on which he works, that men are "like flies"; his ludicrously narcissistic grooming to go out; the cheapness of blind dates ("Why do I always get the girls who look like firehorses?"); his pride in earning $62.50 a week ("more than most college professors"); the untold wealth of $200 won from a bookie. One understands the curl of his lip as he looks over the group gathered to watch him fry.

Three On A Match (1932), set yet again in the familiar Warners world of shopgirls and the rackets, took a less pessimistic view of society, though still retaining implications of moral commentary. Like Van Dyke's *The Devil Is A Sissy*, it insists perhaps overzealously that we are all the same, rich or poor, though in this case the subjects are not slum kids but three girls who lose touch after school, only to meet again as poor stenographer (Bette Davis), wealthy socialite (Ann Dvorak), and notorious showgirl (Joan Blondell). At the end of their reunion lunch, all three light their cigarettes from the same match, then remember the superstition that one will die. Eventually, after some extensive changing of partners — Blondell ending up in Dvorak's place with Davis in tow, Dvorak descending to degradation and death among the mobsters, the pattern is worked out. In a final shot, a

60

cheerful Blondell and Davis light cigarettes and throw the match into the fire.

This is in many ways an unconventional film for LeRoy. The social message is there, but he betrays also a Curtiz-like concern with pace not especially typical of him. There are some neat transitions. Dvorak's quick slide to the gutter is summed up in a brief scene, with two chauffeurs chatting while they wait for their employers to call them. One points out a ragged figure standing on the other side of the street, and confides that she is the woman who used to employ him, his present boss being a girl who, until a year ago, had been a friend of hers. The camera moves in to Dvorak, ashamed and down at heel, then to Blondell leaving the beauty shop. The point is made quickly, and with intelligence, qualities which distinguish LeRoy's sole excursion into the musical during the Thirties, the ebullient and witty *Gold Diggers Of 1933*.

Critics not completely at home with their facts tend to consider the great Warners musicals of the Thirties as little more than Busby Berkeley festivals, the intervening material just spacing to be endured until the next production number. Admittedly Berkeley was a brilliant dance director (his contribution to the period is examined in Chapter 8). He had, however, little effect on the body of the films on which he worked. These belonged to talented Warners directors like Lloyd Bacon, Archie Mayo and Mervyn LeRoy, the work of whom is distinguished enough to be worth considering outside any discussion of Berkeley's dance direction. *Gold Diggers Of 1933* certainly deserves such attention. Few comedy-musicals of the period exhibit so effectively the combination of wit and malice which characterised Warners' humour during the Thirties.

The pattern of *Gold Diggers* is familiar. The heroines — Ruby Keeler, Ginger Rogers, Joan Blondell, Aline MacMahon — are showgirls looking for jobs. Ned Sparks is a producer looking for money. Dick Powell is the playboy song-writer who subsidises Sparks's show, writes and stars in it, and even wins Keeler in the end. The elements of *Forty Second Street* are all there, but rearranged to provide a far more satisfying background. Blondell especially sparkles with the bitterness

61

one expects only from Carole Lombard. Her affair with Warren William, Powell's brother who tries to buy the girls off, is eminently realistic, shot through with some brilliantly scripted exchanges and a genuine feeling of involvement.

Aline MacMahon as the ruthless Trixie, determined to bleed William and his partner (Guy Kibbee) of everything they have, is delightfully opportunist, while Ned Sparks gives a new interpretation of his perennial part of the producer. His passion while planning what will eventually be the "Remember My Forgotten Man" finale is a cleverly acted piece of wry humour. "Men marching, marching," he says in his deadpan whine. He looks into the distance, as towards a promised land of unlimited funds and endless profits. "Jobs, jobs . . . gee, don't it get ya?" The songs are competent, requiring no opulent settings to put them over. In fact, one of the best of them, "I've Got To Sing A Torch Song", is not made the subject of a production number, though a sequence in which Ginger Rogers, in a parody of Helen Morgan, sang it while sitting on a piano, was filmed but never used. In the end, Berkeley's dance numbers seem an imposition on LeRoy's skilful comic pattern; without them, *Gold Diggers* might well be an even more entertaining film than it is now.

As in the case of Curtiz, LeRoy adapted without undue strain to the necessities of Warners' increased prestige in the late Thirties. His work of this period was as much production as direction, indicating the skill that was to take him to Metro at the end of the decade and establish him as a major producer/director. *The World Changes* (1933), with Paul Muni as an industrialist of pioneer stock whose growth as a businessman is paralleled by a loss of contact with his family, unfortunately proves tedious in the extreme, but is competently executed. The film never recovers from its wretched script, an historical grab-bag in which the young Muni manages to meet, purely by accident, every major figure of the period from Custer (who rides in to tell the family that the Civil War is over — they had never known it was on) to Buffalo Bill, who stops by for dinner one night, exhorting Muni to "Go West" and extinguishing at the same time whatever belief one may have had in the feeble story.

By contrast, *Oil For The Lamps Of China* (1935) is far above average in performance, direction and content. A tough and complex study of one man's life spent in the service of a big US oil company in China, it makes a brave attempt to generalise about the conflict between individuality and social allegiance. As the young oil company employee, Pat O'Brien's restrained playing has an appropriate edge of fanaticism, while Josephine Hutchinson as his wife is nicely balanced between wifely pride and despair at "the Company's" all-pervading influence. The film pulls few punches. After a life of devoted service, during which he has sacked his best friend for a minor incompetence, risked his life during the revolution to rescue company funds, and alienated his wife by being absent on company business when their child died, he is passed over for a top job and put in a menial position. His wife pleads for him, and he is given the job at the direction of the company chief who claims to respect O'Brien's contribution to the firm (though one wonders whether the fact that he holds the patent to a lamp the company sells might not have something to do with this decision). The films lacks the sense of the East so apparent in *The Good Earth*, but does suggest in the playing of its actors some of the alien quality of China, the difficulties of adapting to life there, the potential for violence. It is one of the few films of the Thirties to deal exclusively with the problems of work, and the pressures which we in the Sixties are only now beginning to find important enough to write about. In this, it is well ahead of its time.

Among Warners' most ambitious productions was *Anthony Adverse* (1936) from the sprawling Hervey Allen novel of Napoleonic Europe. LeRoy's direction of this project gained the first Oscar for best supporting actress (Gale Sondergaard), as well as others for Best Camerawork (Tony Gaudio), Best Editing (Ralph Dawson) and Best Music (Leo Forbstein for Erich Wolfgang Korngold). It is appropriate that LeRoy should have made this film, because it was his last big production for Warners. In 1938 he went to Metro to become executive producer on *The Wizard Of Oz*, then to make *Waterloo Bridge*, *Blossoms In The Dust* and other Metro money-spinners. His direction of *Anthony Adverse* is, if anything, more competent than any other work of this kind that he did, suggesting a taste for Metro-like glossiness which may explain his decision to change studios. Although episodic and beset by titles, it is, like *Oil For The Lamps Of China*, successful as historical pageant and personal drama, especially interesting for Fredric March's Anthony.

LeRoy's next production, and the second film on which his reputation rests, was *They Won't Forget* (1937), a flawed but essentially tough-minded condemnation of lynch law in the deep South that gives Claude Rains an opportunity to display the talent that had been buried under the foppish character he played in *Anthony Adverse*. As the ambitious small town lawyer determined to become governor by successfully prosecuting an innocent man for the murder of a girl, Rains is convincingly callous and vengeful, throwing himself with vicious glee into the task of getting the death sentence. Prejudice, the myth of the hospitable South, Civil War bitterness; LeRoy marshals all these to enlarge his story. Visually the film is patchy, but some scenes are typical of LeRoy's early Thirties triumphs; a high shot looking directly down on the terrified negro janitor lying on a cell cot surrounded by sweaty cops demanding that he talk; the lynching of the alleged murderer (Edward Norris) suggested by the insane dangle of a mailbag as it is snatched up by the express's hook, the train's roar swamping his cries; Lana Turner's corpse crumpled at the bottom of a lift shaft, illuminated fitfully by the probing light of torches. The refusal to mitigate the mob's act by suggesting, as did Lang's *Fury*, that lynchers are only human, gives it a typical LeRoy tone of righteous anger. There is no forgiveness, he suggests, for people like Rains, least of all from their own consciences. They won't forget, and nor do we.

It would have been appropriate for LeRoy to close his career at Warners on this note, but Hollywood seldom supplies a neat ending. His last film for Warners was the routine *Fools For Scandal* (1938), interesting for its French star, Fernand Gravet, but for little else.

Warners expertise at its most ingenious. Careful lighting of a simple set injects drama into this shot of Edward G. Robinson in Mervyn LeRoy's LITTLE CAESAR.

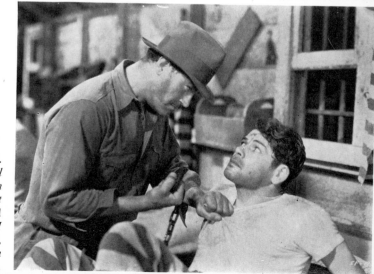

Edward J. McNamara and Paul Muni in a scene from a Warners protest film, I AM A FUGITIVE FROM A CHAIN GANG, directed by Mervyn LeRoy.

An economical and effective Chinese set design typical of Warners in the Thirties amplifies the performances of Pat O'Brien and Josephine Hutchinson in Mervyn LeRoy's OIL FOR THE LAMPS OF CHINA

Victor Jory as Oberon and Anita Louise as Titania the William Dieterle/Max Reinhardt version A MIDSUMMER NIGHT'S DREAM

After this squib, LeRoy went to Metro, where he was to establish himself, financially at least, as a major force in Forties' cinema. His first film there, *Dramatic School* (1938), is an interesting amalgam of two or three different styles, notable mainly for the performance of Luise Rainer, who proved, despite the contrary evidence of *The Great Ziegfeld* (the best possible argument against the view that Oscars for acting mean anything), that she was capable of effective work on the screen. Her portrait of the young actress almost insanely devoted to becoming a star is among the most coherent any performer of the Thirties achieved.

The story is an uneasy combination of the omnibus tradition — *Grand Hotel, Dinner At Eight* — and the romantic comedy which Paramount made its speciality, but the attempt to show the drama that goes on inside a Paris dramatic school eventually contracts to a study of Luise Rainer and her struggles to stay alive long enough to be discovered. Rainer perfectly suggests the intensity of a born actress, her pale, almost consumptive face giving her a ghostly presence, enhanced by her breathy, accented voice. We sense an hysterical idealism behind her habit of inventing elaborate fantasies to obscure the fact that she works in a factory all night to pay for tuition. One scene sums it up perfectly. A variety star and her party breeze into the factory at night to "gather material". Her valuable bracelet is lost, Rainer accused of stealing it. Found caught in the star's dress, it is offered shamefaced to her as a conciliatory gift. The exhausted, down-at-heel girl smiles cheerfully at the elegantly dressed star and shakes her head. "Thank you," she says, "but I never wear jewellery." That he should have wrung so moving and truthful a performance from an actress apparently limited in talent is a fitting end to Mervyn LeRoy's rich Thirties' career.

After Curtiz and LeRoy, the pantheon of Warners' directors becomes confused. There can be no doubt, however, that among the best of its technicians was another German import, **WILLIAM DIETERLE**. Ex-actor (Leni's *Waxworks*) and a former student of Max Reinhardt, he built in the Thirties a sound technical competence that was to carry

65

him through a distinguished Forties career during which he created such masterpieces as *Portrait of Jennie*, *All That Money Can Buy* and *Love Letters*. All his films are marked by a Teutonic thoroughness and control, undiluted, however, with the imagination of Curtiz. Only in the Forties did he achieve the mastery of actors and lighting which allowed his meticulous sense of atmosphere full range. His earlier work occasionally achieves it, but is more often only sporadically exciting.

Her Majesty, Love (1931), a sex comedy in the Lubitsch style copied from a German success has remained famous only for the appearance in it of the nihilistic W. C. Fields and a rare part by the almost legendary Ziegfeld star Marilyn Miller. Fields's performance at a formal dinner is a sequence still included in anthologies; beginning with a simple request from a man at the other end of the table to pass an éclair, the scene has Fields flipping pastries with impeccable aim to land on a plate fifteen feet away, juggling dishes and entertaining the company with details of his barbering business and his daughter's work as a barmaid. Many of the settings are seedy, and lit with Germanic ruthlessness. Veteran Leon Errol is engaging as the flagging aristocrat feeding up on oysters and champagne with eggs in it before tackling his seventh wife, but it is the melancholy Fields who leaves his mark indelibly on the film.

In *Scarlet Dawn* (1932), another Russian revolution story, Douglas Fairbanks Jnr. and the singularly untalented Nancy Carroll act out the unlikely tale of an exiled aristocrat and serving girl who eventually overcome the barriers of class distinction and marry. Two features lift it above the average — Anton Grot's ornate Russian settings, and the sexually charged nature of the material. The first shows a von Sternberg influence, especially in the Fairbanks villa in Moscow, with its interlocking arches and chunky beams. Statues loom in the foreground as revolutionary soldiers ransack the house; the rooms are rich with *objets d'art*, icons, draperies. Equally compelling is the sordid Turkish kitchen where the fugitive Fairbanks secures a job washing dishes, and the Greek Orthodox church in which, with a Parisian whore and a German tailor as witnesses, he is married to his ex-maid.

Far more striking, however, is the film's attention to sexual detail. As the Russian Army officer homeward bound to "feather beds and accommodating women", Fairbanks is charmingly promiscuous, his first encounter with his mistress (Lilyan Tashman) believably brutal. Bursting into her apartment he begins immediately to strip. The astonished Tashman comes from an inner bedroom, closing the door hastily behind her in a sign that she has not been alone, and is immediately locked in an embrace which reaches its logical conclusion, one imagines, on the floor. A few moments later a brief orgy sequence evokes lust and decadence more effectively than any other film of the period. Sprawled in a disordered room watching frantic cossack dancers, the officers cuddle and caress their semi-naked women; some of the girls receive the attention of two men at once, another lies in an erotic daze, staring heavy-eyed into the camera as her lover busies himself at some indistinguishable pastime in the bed behind her. The amoral tone of *Scarlet Dawn* is summed up in a later conversation between Fairbanks, an inept gigolo in Istanbul, and Tashman, who has changed her way of life only to the extent of now satisfying the needs of a commissar instead of a prince. Fairbanks taxes her with this situation, but is assured that she has no feeling for her new protector. "I'm glad", he remarks lightly, "Morals never bothered me too much but taste is *so* important." Ruthlessly edited, with skilful use of wipes, this is one of the period's most unusual films.

One might say the same of *A Midsummer Night's Dream* (1935), the adaptation of Shakespeare which Dieterle co-directed with his old teacher Max Reinhardt. It is hard to ascertain what part Dieterle played in making this film; though the European richness of imagery and mood is inescapably that of Reinhardt, the overall tone of the film is dark in the Dieterle style. The saturnine figure of Victor Jory's Oberon, a sinister presence in many scenes, is typical, more so when he is "disguised" as a tree, little more than a gnarled shape from which his face peers enigmatically. Undoubtedly Dieterle is also responsible for the effective use made of the complex forest sets; the gloomy mood which he achieves provides the best possible background for the shimmering Anita Louise as Titania and such spectacles of special effects as the fairies' weaving of a web of sleep over their Queen. Doubts about the allocation of credit for the Dieterle/Reinhardt film remain, although more information is now available. The film's source was the 1927 Reinhardt Broadway production (in German) which toured widely in Europe and was presented in English at the Hollywood Bowl with a cast that included its eventual star Olivia de Havilland. Since the film was based on this well-established production the ruling visual conception is clearly Reinhardt's, though Hal Mohr, who received a special Oscar for his lighting, has characterised both Reinhardt and Dieterle as vague about the film's staging, and emphasised his own considerable contribution. However much one may question the wisdom of casting in this difficult play such doubtful talents as Dick Powell, James Cagney and Mickey Rooney, its assurance as a work of film technique is undoubted. As in so many other Thirties' films, form triumphantly obliterates content.

Towards the end of the period, Dieterle had, like Curtiz and LeRoy, his share of "prestige" projects, and made of them the competent job one would have expected. *The Story Of Louis Pasteur* (1936) *The Life Of Emile Zola* (1937) and *Juarez* (1939) were all Paul Muni vehicles, dignified by his commanding presence and skilful make-up, marred by his habit of padding parts and hogging the stage. Probably more worthy of comment was *Another Dawn* (1937), a fevered story of forbidden love in a British desert outpost gaining little from the presence of a triangle made up of Errol Flynn, Kay Francis and Ian Hunter. Something is, however, suggested of the *cafard* induced by desert life, the enervating heat, and the boredom which engenders sexual attraction.

Dieterle's triumph, however, was a production made for RKO but exhibiting all the marks of Warners' best films. *The Hunchback Of Notre Dame* (1939) has seldom been bettered as an evocation of medieval life, while Charles Laughton's portrayal of the grotesque Quasimodo makes even that of Lon Chaney seem feeble. The early sequences are of an unbelievable detail and intensity. Cavorting before the bulk of Notre Dame among Van Nest Polglase's brilliant carnival sets, the people of Paris are exhibited in a Breughel-like pageant of vulgarity and violence. Crippled beggars scuttle, tumblers bounce, a young playwright (Edmond O'Brien) has his gloomy masque of death and retribution interrupted by the apparition of Quasimodo's hideous face thrust through a paper rose window at the back of the stage to hang there leering stupidly, its deformity capped by an incongruous jester's crown.

The atmosphere of ignorance, superstition and terror is sustained in Laughton's later appearances, especially that in which he is led at the stirrup of his master through crowds which shrink back as he waddles by, his precious crown dangling from one hand. Seeing their fear, he turns and circles threateningly around — instantly the watchers melt away. There is an element of almost supernatural horror also in O'Brien's descent into the subterranean kingdom of thieves, grasping deformed figures in the shadows driving him to where the king of the beggars (Thomas Mitchell) presides. A one-legged man limps in, relaxes, and magically unfolds a whole limb from under his rags; another, blind, gropes into the light, and the young poet watches in terror as the blank eyes suddenly become alive again, and drop to count the money in the cup. Even Quasimodo's final orgy of destruction, in which he rains down molten lead, beams and stones on the besieging mob, does not exceed in grotesquerie these early scenes.

It is because of its realism and devotion to sexual and social detail that Warners is an interesting studio for modern writers on cinema. Its films are often indistinguishable from the more effective television dramas, and their callousness is particularly in tune with the disenchanted Sixties; in mood and ethos Godard is closer to Curtiz than to any other American director. One would like to spend more time examining the work of men like Curtiz and LeRoy as well as others, such as Alfred E. Green, whose films were both typical and individual. The difficulty, however, of fitting all these men into one section suggests the amount of material which exists in the Warners' output of the Thirties, a field other researchers might sift with profit.

5. Fantasy: Universal and Elsewhere

NO SINGLE aspect of its cinema reflects so accurately a country's preoccupations as that of fantasy. However obscure may be the motivations of its comedy or drama, the injection into films of any supernatural element reveals its deepest preoccupations and psychoses. From country to country there is a distinct variation in fantastic themes, approaches and degrees of commitment, crystallised in the form of a set of fantasy elements carried forward with little alteration from the earliest literature of the nation through its drama and dance to final use in an art which combines all these forms, the cinema.

American cinema is no exception to this rule. Even in its brief and derivative artistic progress the United States has formed a set of fantasy elements that exhibit themselves in its ghost, horror and science fiction films. In general, however, the history of American fantasy cinema has been one of influence and absorption; the lumbering gait of Wegener's *Der Golem* (1913) is duplicated by Boris Karloff in James Whale's *Frankenstein* (1931), Ricou Browning in Jack Arnold's *The Creature Walks Among Us* (1956) and even the charming Robby the Robot in Fred Wilcox's *Forbidden Planet* (1956), just as the waxworks motif in Leni's *Das Wachsfigurenkabinett* (1924) appears in Michael Curtiz's *Mystery Of The Wax Museum* (1933) and frequently thereafter in such films as *The Florentine Dagger* (1935) and *House of Wax* (1953). Although elements from many other countries were adopted by American film-makers, notably the concept of wish-fulfilling dreams from the French, it is mainly from German sources that the inspiration for American fantasy films is drawn. Few productions have succeeded which were not deeply embedded in the ambience of German Gothic, and the fantasies of mutilation and tyranny which are central to the Teutonic psyche.

The best fantasy film-makers were Europeans who combined a knowledge of the Germanic temperament with a mastery of American technique. Many were imported by Carl Laemmle of Universal

Studios, a man who in the Twenties had done well out of the eccentric by backing Erich von Stroheim in his most successful productions. It was Laemmle who imported German director Paul Leni to make, among other films, the prestigious and profitable *The Cat And The Canary* (1927), and who provided the opportunity for three of the best horror film directors, James Whale, Karl Freund and Tod Browning, to create their masterpieces. Universal was not primarily a horror film studio, and in fact only a tiny percentage of its output was devoted to this form; that its more disreputable productions should be remembered today long after the work of polished directors like John Stahl has faded is another of Hollywood's wry jokes.

There is no director of horror films in the history of the cinema who so completely explored and mastered the medium as Englishman **JAMES WHALE**, Universal's "Ace" and the creator of three key films in the genre, *Frankenstein*, *The Invisible Man* and *The Old Dark House*. Imported along with star Colin Clive to direct the R. C. Sherriff war drama *Journey's End*, which he had produced, designed and bought part of in Britain, but which primitive sound systems made it impossible to film there, he turned out during his Hollywood career a handful of elegant British-influenced melodramas and four great horror films. The former have been largely forgotten, though it is unfortunate that Colin Clive's convincing portrait of an officer physically and mentally ravaged by war in *Journey's End* (1930) should have passed from sight, and that the Paramount-like softness and elegance of *Show Boat* (1936) with its great performances by Paul Robeson and Helen Morgan is now almost unknown. There is, in fact, ample evidence to suggest that, despite their quality, Whale's horror films are not especially typical of him. Almost without exception their tone is that of the half-disguised spoof, and a thread of black humour runs through all of them, mocking material and audience alike.

Frankenstein (1931) is still the most famous of all horror films, and deservedly so. Boris Karloff as the lumbering monster produces, with the aid of Jack Pierce's make-up (see Chapter 8) and gestures obtained via Chaney and Wegener, a moving example of tragic mime, his awkward movements and inarticulate grunts inducing in the audience an almost instant sympathy. There is genuine feeling in sequences such as the monster's visit to the blind anchorite who hides him when he is pursued, unaware of his guest's monstrous shape, and a sort of maniac elation, assisted by some startling special effects, in the vivifying of the newly-constructed creature. Despite this, however, one cannot help finding the operetta-style Tyrolean village setting somewhat disconcerting and the presence in the cast of characters like Lionel Belmore's crotchety burgomaster an invitation to levity.

In *The Old Dark House* (1932) adapted from J. B. Priestley's "Benighted", the humour, though buried, is still apparent. An exercise in the tradition of *The Cat And The Canary*, and incorporating such Leni effects as a corridor lined with billowing curtains, it builds carefully to a series of cynically engineered anti-climaxes. The group stranded in the ancient mansion, including a plus-foured north country Charles Laughton in his first American film, is initially introduced to a rogue's gallery of sinister types — lecherous, brutish butler (Boris Karloff), pyromaniac dwarf (Brember Wills), Ernest Thesiger and Eva Moore as an insane brother and sister. Karloff's lust for Gloria Stewart, Laughton's mistress, the sinister glinting of the knife which carves the roast, and a variety of veiled hints at "somebody upstairs" prepare us for a night of rape and murder, but each threat as it appears is revealed to be burlap and poster paint. The arsonist, heralded by the terrifying appearance of a withered hand on the banister, is gnomish and shy, his secluded companion in the upper storeys an aged relative of 102 with little potential for mayhem. Despite storm, attempted rape and a remarkable final chase, the film is basically a confidence trick worked with cynical humour by a brilliant technician.

Even more effective an exercise in technique, *The Invisible Man* (1933) sustains the *comédie noire* mood of earlier Whale fantasies. Claude Rains, giving what amounts to a radio performance — he becomes visible only when dead, a dramatically satisfying if scientifically ridiculous climax — raves and rages in a convincing description of megalomania, providing an unusual contrast to the aplomb of the average horror film hero. His games with the police, the elaborate editing which provides wry contrasts between many of the scenes, even the dénouement in which Rains's plans are upset by the early snow and he is trapped by his own footprints suggest the work of what is basically a comic talent.

These three films represent Whale's pioneering efforts in the field. Each is the exploration of what is, by American standards at least, a new idea, examining with a fresh and inventive eye the possibilities of an unfamiliar form. With *The Bride Of Frankenstein* (1935), Whale began to repeat himself, and it is perhaps because he was by now master of the horror film that this production is the best of them all. There is the same wit, inculcated mainly by the playing of Whale's old friend Ernest Thesiger as Dr. Praetorius, a sinister hermit brooding over his collection of human miniatures, including a bride and groom reduced on their wedding night and never since allowed to touch one another, and an even more heightened atmosphere of Ruritanian decay and superstition. The prologue, with Elsa Lanchester playing Mary Shelley, author of "Frankenstein", does not entirely prepare us for her appearance as the bride which Frankenstein and Praetorius create for the monster, but the momentary invitation to laugh is stifled by her magnificent performance as the awakening creature, quick, twitchy bird-like movements of the head and low-angle shooting by John Mescall to show the scars on her throat emphasising her alien quality, the white streak in her bush of hair providing a sort of visual exclamation mark to our surprise. Whale the satirist here perhaps succumbed to Whale the fantasist, and the result is a striking moment of the cinema.

Just as competent as Whale but less inclined to guy his material, **TOD BROWNING** directed for Universal and later for Metro a number of the decade's most intriguing horror films. An ex-vaudeville comic, actor, scriptwriter and assistant to D. W. Griffith, he had a natural affinity for the melodramatic and grotesque which made him the logical choice to direct the great character actor and make-up artist Lon Chaney. In the Twenties, he handled such Chaney vehicles as *The*

Unholy Three (1925), *The Road To Mandalay* (1926) and *London After Midnight* (1927). Browning had hoped to use Chaney in *Dracula,* but the actor died in August 1930, just after completing work on his first sound film, a remake by Jack Conway of his 1925 success *The Unholy Three,* and Browning had to use the Hungarian Bela Lugosi, who played the role on Broadway.

Dracula (1931), like so many other horror films of the period, is remembered primarily for a handful of scenes which exceed the remainder in quality and atmosphere. The early sequences as Dwight Frye arrives in the superstition-ridden Transylvanian village have a cumulative gloom far more successfully handled than in Murnau's *Nosferatu,* while the interiors of Dracula's castle, with its dust-clogged cobwebs and the howls of wolves drifting from the forest ("Children of the night; what music they make!"), are effectively Gothic. Browning's London, as photographed by Karl Freund, is a fog-swathed city of ghosts, the damp and chill emphasised by the cellar in which Dracula hides, a musty vault among whose Gothic arches his three mistresses creep like creatures found under a stone. Unfortunately, the stage origins of this version of Bram Stoker's novel show through, especially in Lugosi's inept acting, and it is only the visual material which contains any suggestion of the original's intensity.

After making *The Iron Man* (1931), a boxing drama with Lew Ayres based on a novel by W. R. Burnett, Browning left Universal and joined Metro. M-G-M appears frequently in the Thirties as a producer of horror films, and, as well as Browning, Karl Freund became a regular staff member later in the decade. It is a paradox that one of the cheapest of Hollywood studios, Universal, and the most prosperous, Metro, should have been almost equally responsible for the great horror films of the period.

Browning had been hired by Metro to make a more ambitious version of the many successful circus films then being produced. Characteristically, he took as his subject not a conventional drama of life under the big top but a cynical story called "Spurs" by fantasy writer Tod Robbins. *Freaks* (1932), though criticised today for its excess of melodrama, is still one of the great grotesques. Harry Earles, the dwarf (he had played the "baby" in Conway's *The Unholy Three*), is a circus midget whose money makes him the prey of Olga Baclanova, the beautiful performer who, with her lumbering strong-man boyfriend, is one of the few normal people in the film, most of the remainder being deformed. One senses that *Freaks* is in many ways a glimpse of another world where physical shape is unimportant. In the culminating sequence as the freaks writhe and scramble through the mud to hunt down the two who have killed their fellow, their clogged bodies seem briefly formless, as if losing even their vague relationship to human shape. The emasculation of the strong-man (deleted from some versions of this film) and the crushing of Baclanova into the hideous "chicken woman" seen squatting in a bran pit in the final shot mean that the only two "normal" people in the film become at the end freaks too, and "reality" is restored.

Mark Of The Vampire (1935), a remake of the Chaney success *London After Midnight* (1927), was not especially successful, but *The Devil Doll* (1936) is still one of the Thirties' most effective examples of atmospheric fantasy. The characteristic Browning elements — greed as a motive, transvestism — reappear in the story of an escaped convict who is given the secret of reducing human beings to miniatures and uses it to revenge himself on the men who put him on Devil's Island. The idea of miniaturisation is used with more drama in this film than in others of its kind, and the attacks which Lionel Barrymore engineers, hiding outside disguised as an old woman while controlling his mannikins telepathically, are directed with eerie skill; a tiny man waking to find himself hung from the Christmas tree with a floppy bow around his chest, a woman who wriggles from the arms of a sleeping child and creeps along the edge of a bed to sink her drugged stiletto into the throat of her victim.

Browning, like Whale, was a painstaking worker with a detailed knowledge of cinema technique. This skill, allied to a genuine feeling for the grotesque, gave him the ability to create convincing horror films, though not as convincing as those of a yet greater technician and one of the best directors of fantasy films in the Thirties, the German **KARL FREUND**. As a cameraman, Freund is famous; his work on *The Last Laugh, Metropolis* and *Variety* in Germany was followed by some of the most beautiful lighting ever achieved in Hollywood, notably on *The Good Earth, Camille*, Browning's *Dracula* and Florey's *Murders In The Rue Morgue*, films in which he showed his mastery of the techniques of lighting for fantasy. His directorial career is a brief one, spanning eight films, but the first (for Universal) and the last (for Metro) of these are both fantasies as beautiful and strange as any ever produced.

Boris Karloff's awakening in *The Mummy* (1932) is among the most terrifying scenes in any horror film, but it is only part of a masterly two-part characterisation, as Imhotep, the Egyptian priest condemned to living death for his attempt to resurrect a dead princess, and the impeccably sinister Ardath Bey, the persona Imhotep assumes after his accidental revival. Opening with the discovery by an expedition of Karloff's tomb, it moves with dark intensity through some of the most Gothic of all horror scenes; the mummy's revivification, its crusted eyes creeping open as Bramwell Fletcher reads the scroll on which the spell is inscribed, the slow extending of a bandaged hand with fragments of rubbish trembling on the fingertips to suggest the rotting nature of the body, an exit shown by unravelled bandages dragging across the tomb's floor as Fletcher's insane laughter echoes around its walls; Karloff recalling his sacrilege, ancient Egypt floating up out of the pool before him as he murmurs, "I knelt by the bed of death"; an ending with Zita Johann being saved from mummification by a prayer to Isis which causes Karloff to crumble horribly to a dusty skeleton. Editing (Milton Carruth) very much in the Germanic style, magnificent lighting credited to Charles Stumar (but pure Freund) and a superb performance from Karloff make this a fantasy almost without equal.

Like *The Mummy*, Freund's last fantasy, *Mad Love* (1934) deals extensively in the familiar currency of German Gothic. The characteristic horror of physical injury, and especially of dismemberment, occupies a central part in this adaptation of *The Hands Of Orlac*, a

Maurice Renard novel already filmed once in Germany by Robert Wiene in 1924. As in such fantasy classics as *Das Wachsfigurenkabinett* and *The Beast With Five Fingers* it is the severing of a hand which is given prominence, and the fact that Stephen Orlac, whose hands are minced in a train accident, is a concert pianist adds to the particular horror of the film. Playing Gogol, the sinister surgeon who, in order to ingratiate himself with Orlac's beautiful wife, grafts onto the pianist's stumps the hands of a guillotined knife murderer, Peter Lorre in his first American film oozes the vicious sadism which made his work in Lang's *M* so effective. Photographed by Chester Lyons, assisted by Gregg Toland, who spent eight days on the film, *Mad Love* is nevertheless visually as typical of Freund as his shadowy Universal fantasy. Pop-eyed, baby-faced and bald, Lorre is one of the few actors able to suggest with any conviction the necrophilic sadism of Gogol. In the Grand Guignol which he visits every night to see Frances Drake branded on the wheel in a fantasy of medieval torture, the lighting floods one half of his obscenely smooth head but leaves the rest in total dark, suggesting the balance of sanity and madness inside the egg-like skull. Most macabre of all, however, is the sequence in which Orlac visits an abandoned apartment to meet, he is led to believe, the man whose hands he now has. Hidden in the dark, the occupant, on being ordered to prove his identity, thrusts under the lamp two articulated steel gauntlets laced with leather straps. "But your head," Orlac says incredulously. "They cut it off. . . ." The other leans forward to show a metal collar enclosing his throat and lower face. "Yes," the voice says quietly, "but Gogol sewed it on again." The logical resolution of *Mad Love,* with Gogol unmasked as the "revived" murderer, cannot dispel the horror of this moment nor lighten the unease which it evokes in its audience.

Some of Freund's most effective camerawork was in *Murders In The Rue Morgue* (1932), yet another Universal adaptation of a European fantasy classic, directed by the Frenchman **ROBERT FLOREY**. Originally chosen to direct *Frankenstein* with Bela Lugosi as the monster, Florey was distressed when James Whale's reputation and the indifferent quality of screen tests shot with Lugosi encouraged

Laemmle to take this project out of their hands. The suggestion that Florey and Lugosi were given Poe's story as a consolation prize has encouraged most critics to look on *Murders In The Rue Morgue* as unworthy of interest, though the quality of Lugosi's performance as Doctor Mirakle in this film, contrasted with the cheap melodrama of his mime when he did eventually play the Frankenstein monster (*Frankenstein Meets The Wolf Man*, 1942) suggests that the cinema gained from the re-allocation of talent.

Florey's re-creation of Paris in 1845 is perfunctory in the extreme, owing more to medieval Germany than post-Napoleonic France. The carnival with which the film opens and the sideshow of Doctor Mirakle are pure Caligari, even to Lugosi's high hat and ulster, and the somnambulistic character of his servant (Noble Johnson). Inside the tent, patrons listen spellbound as Mirakle exhibits a huge gorilla and expounds, with the aid of grotesque charts, his mad theory of evolution, though their interest turns quickly to horror as he hints at his experiments in injecting gorilla blood into humans. Close-ups of their frightened, angry faces combined here as in other scenes with quick cutting suggest the violence underlying their fascination, leading us naturally to Mirakle's insane kidnapping of a prostitute and the fatal operation which he performs on her. A French flippancy shows up in Florey's employment of "light relief" — a frothy picnic, some heavy-handed humour where the witnesses to a murder speculate on whether the killer (Mirakle's ape) spoke German, Danish or Italian — but the Teutonic nature of the playing, sets and quasi-medical detail cannot be denied.

The greatest Florey film is undoubtedly *The Beast With Five Fingers* (1947), but many of his conventional programme pictures show elements and influences of German Gothic. *Dangerous To Know* (1938), one of his Paramount low-life melodramas with Akim Tamiroff, has an eccentric ending reminiscent of Peter Lorre's organ-playing climax in *Mad Love*, mobster Tamiroff ecstatically pumping out Tchaikovsky oblivious of his mistress (Anna May Wong) disembowelling herself behind him. Another thriller, *The Florentine Dagger* (Warners, 1935) combines a cynical Ben Hecht story with atmospheric images in the style of the more sophisticated German horror films. Donald Woods, as the last of the Borgias, returns to the ancestral castle to poison himself in an eccentric homage to family history. Dissuaded from this course by a Broadway entrepreneur (Henry O'Neill), he writes a play about Lucrezia Borgia to feature O'Neill's daughter (Margaret Lindsay), falls for the star and is then implicated in O'Neill's murder, a stabbing carried out with a Borgia dagger. There are some suspenseful knife assaults by black-gloved figures and a remarkable *dénouement* in a mask-maker's shop where (shades of *Mystery Of The Wax Museum*) the murderer is revealed to be one of the cast who has hidden a fire-scarred face for years behind a realistic wax mask, but the film is at best a footnote to a confused Thirties' career.

Another Universal import, the Austrian **EDGAR ULMER**, created one of the most interesting yet least typical horror films of the Thirties. *The Black Cat* (1934), despite a credit claiming it was "suggested by Edgar Allen [sic] Poe's masterpiece", is a modern fantasy with none of the Poe grotesquerie, even the black cat which provides an excuse for the title having no observable relationship to the plot. Characteristically, the film is another excursion into the Ulmer mystique, its people moved by motivations rooted in abstract attitudes of mind, concepts of duty and revenge so complex as to defy analysis. The setting is a futuristic castle built by engineer Boris Karloff on the ruins of the fort he commanded (and surrendered to the enemy) during the war, and in the cellars of which he holds meetings of an antichristian sect. Returning to Karloff's eyrie after fifteen years as a prisoner of war, Dr. Vitos Verdigast (Bela Lugosi) finds that his daughter (Lucille Lund) has become Karloff's mistress, while his wife's body has been preserved as a trophy in the vaults of the fortress, filling only one of the many glass cases Karloff has there.

Although Peter Ruric's script incorporates into the story a selection of Gothic elements — Karloff's necrophilia, the finale in which Lugosi flays Karloff alive — the ambience is far from Germanic, suggesting rather a dream-like state owing little to national characteristics. **Ulmer** uses reflections and veils to diffuse the image; during an operation, a glass bowl seems to glow supernaturally; a tree snapped off in a motor accident falls through the rain as if weightless; Karloff and his blonde mistress sleep in a bed swathed in veils, cherished creatures of some obscure reality. One finds it difficult to reconcile with this world of dreams the concrete caverns in which the climax is set, their forme-marked walls suggesting a universe closer to Le Corbusier than Le Fanu, leaning crosses in Karloff's aseptic chapel hinting at some dark variation on Christianity in which his mysticism takes root. Ulmer's career is tangled, but on the basis of this film alone he would deserve to be considered among the masters.

However rich in invention the work of Universal may have become, it was characterised always by the sparsity of its physical materials. While its films are often exciting and individual, their quality stems invariably from superior lighting and resourceful use of simple cheap sets. This combination accounted for most of Universal's great fantasies, and for the superior productions in this field which it engineered in the Forties and Fifties, specifically the work of Jack Arnold, whose manipulation of atmosphere and illusion in such films as *The Incredible Shrinking Man* and *Creature From The Black Lagoon* makes him Whale's natural successor. Today as in all periods, however, the cheap, atmospheric product of Universal suffers commercially by comparison with the glossy output of studios like Metro, and it is predictable that, in the Thirties, Universal found itself defeated at the box office by fantasies and grotesques which made up in superior sets and stars for their deficiences in imagination.

Two of Metro's horror films deserve consideration as examples of fantasy at its most entertaining. Charles Brabin's *The Mask Of Fu Manchu* (1932), with a script contributed to by John Willard, author of the original *The Cat And The Canary*, gives us Boris Karloff in a role far removed in exotic detail if not in style from his Universal triumphs. In determined pursuit of the lost tomb of Genghis Khan where he hopes to find a great mask which will give him power over all Asia, Fu tortures and kills with reckless disregard for all but his ambition.

Top, Elsa Lanchester as the monster's artificial bride and Colin Clive as Doctor Frankenstein in James Whale's THE BRIDE OF FRANKENSTEIN. Centre, Bela Lugosi as Count Dracula in Tod Browning's DRACULA. Below, Bela Lugosi as Doctor Mirakle in Robert Florey's MURDERS IN THE RUE MORGUE.

Left, the personification of Oriental menace and evil: Boris Karloff as Fu Manchu in THE MASK OF FU MANCHU. Right (top), a vision of hell from DANTE'S INFERNO, based on Gustave Doré's engravings; and (bottom) a distorted Bela Lugosi and Doctor Frankenstein's heir (Basil Rathbone) discuss methods of awakening the quiescent monster (Boris Karloff) in SON OF FRANKENSTEIN.

His methods include binding a victim under a huge bell, tormenting him both with vibrations and with the promise of food artfully withheld a few inches from the parched lips, as well as treating others with a serum extracted from the venom of the reptiles he keeps in his laboratory. After a kidnapping in the British Museum with his henchmen dressed as mummies, Fu's pursuit of the mask ends in the desert where a gang of sweating labourers uncovers in the night a set of beaten metal doors on which, in a style reminiscent of Tutankhamen's tomb, images of threatening warriors bar the way. Inside, seated crookedly on a raised throne, the skeleton of Genghis Khan, magnificent in armour, looks terrifyingly down; the helmet is dragged off, the vital half-mask plucked away to reveal a white skull from the eye-socket of which a spider scuttles like the great murderer's fleeing ghost.

More specific in its violence, William Cowan's *Kongo* (1932) gains from superior camerawork (Harold Rosson) and a distinguished cast dominated by Walter Huston re-creating the part of Flint played in the 1928 version (*West Of Zanzibar*, Tod Browning) by Lon Chaney. As the paralysed ruler of a black empire in the Congo, Huston seethes visibly with a desire to revenge himself on the man who broke his back and then, standing over him, sneered. On a piece of paper he has written the words "He sneered", under which he marks off the months until he can begin his revenge on the man's daughter (Virginia Bruce). At the appointed time, Huston's henchman takes the girl from the convent in which she is secluded, and conveys her not to her father but to a brothel in Zanzibar, where she becomes a prostitute and alcoholic. It is only when Flint discovers the girl is not his enemy's daughter but his own that he repents and sacrifices himself to the natives in order to let her and her lover escape.

The detail of Huston's authority over the natives is effectively depicted, especially the scene in which his servant lurches out of the swamp enveloped in a hideous mask with balefully flashing eyes, an apparition before which the tribe flees; around the feet of the shambling creature huge spiders, lizards and crocodiles thrash out of the slime as if they too are terrified (this scene was almost certainly taken intact from *West of Zanzibar*). Few Hollywood films are so relentless in their sadism: Huston's torture of his mistress, Lupe Velez, is to twist her tongue with a loop of wire, while her lover, addicted to an exotic drug, is immersed to his neck in the swamp "to let the leeches suck it out of him." Cedric Gibbons's sets, with their complementary textures of bamboo and human bones, add yet more atmosphere. The cruelty is not, however, without a sick humour. Dragging himself out of his wheelchair, the crippled, unshaven Huston thrusts his scarred face into that of Velez and demands, "Have you ever of all the men you have known seen such an Adonis?" while, in an earlier scene, about to suffer a spinal operation without anaesthetic, he asks, "Will this hurt?" "Yes," the doctor says. "Then give me a cigar."

Occasionally, Hollywood was diverted from the catalogue of Germanic horrors to approach, almost always tangentially and largely by accident, fields of fantasy based on the work of one particular artist. The exquisite fragment *Salome* (1922), with décor based on the drawings of Aubrey Beardsley, was such a film, but an even less well known work is Harry Lachman's *Dante's Inferno* (1935), a Fox production containing some of the most startling special effects work of the period, inspired by Gustav Doré's illustrations for Dante's poem. William Fox had made a previous version of this subject in 1924, but even with the extensive re-creations of demoniac torture, adaptation by Edmund Goulding and some explicit sadism and nudity heightened by the use of tinted film stock, it had little to recommend it. The 1935 version, both for its special effects and the nature of the framing story, is one of the most unusual and effectively presented films of the Thirties.

Spencer Tracy is a stoker who leaves his boat and gets a carnival job, target in a game where people throw balls at his head and win prizes for hitting him. The owner (Henry B. Walthall) of an almost defunct exhibit called "Dante's Inferno" befriends the belligerent Tracy, placing him in charge of his tatty show with its dusty paintings and sculptures intended to convince people of the worthlessness of power and the temporal world. Tracy makes it into a hit, touting and exaggerating in a way dramatised by a dissolve from the portrait of Alexander The Great to Tracy in the same pose, wearing the same helmet, heckling a crowd about the "genuine" nature of the relics he displays. Further shots show him with devils looming over him, and a black owl stares moodily down as he expounds to the other carnies the virtues of consolidating all their shows into one, an enormous Dante's Inferno that will "put hell on a paying basis". He receives their assent, but not before he has married carny girl Claire Trevor in an odd ceremony reminiscent of *Freaks*, with the organ-grinder's monkey as her maid of honour.

The Inferno, when built, is a towering edifice entered through the belly of a crouching swivel-eyed devil. Visitors descend in a spiral, staring either at the tableaux of horror presented on one side or the seething pit they can see far below them at the bottom of the central well. The project, however, seems cursed. On the opening night, an exhibitor who has been put out of business by the ruthless Tracy throws himself into the pit, and a few months later, on the night of a charity gala, the whole construction collapses because of faulty workmanship. In hospital, he is visited by Walthall, who describes to him the vision he had of Dante and the catalogue of horrors recorded in his poem. In a coma, Tracy has a dream of hell which re-creates with astonishing accuracy a series of Doré's engravings; naked bodies jut from boiling pits of fire, battalions of writhing souls toil up mountains of black rock, a nude girl is forced down into a fiery cell by a pivoting lid of stone which she struggles vainly to hold back. Later, Tracy opens a gambling ship, but this too is destroyed by fire, though he redeems himself by beaching it and saving the passengers. Designed by Willy Pogany, who also did Freund's *The Mummy,* photographed by Rudolph Maté, making his first American film, with early uses of the zoom and overhead tracking shots in a shipboard sequence featuring a young dancer named Rita Cansino (later Hayworth), this is a film which deserves greater attention as one of the more lavish examples of fantastic cinema.

Equally competent, but far better known, are the two "monster" films made by Ernest B. Schoedsack, *King Kong* (1932), and *Son Of Kong*

(1933). These fantasies on the survival of prehistoric creatures in a modern urban civilisation are direct results, as was *Dante's Inferno*, of the imagination of one man, though in this case he did not merely inspire but contributed substantially to the production. Willis O'Brien, who created the special effects for both these films, as well as for *The Lost World* (1927), their predecessor, and *Mighty Joe Young* (1949), the modern sequel which finally earned him recognition for his work, is one of the great geniuses of fantasy cinema, and the man directly responsible for the "monster" genre. Without his meticulously constructed and animated scale models, Schoedsack's films could not have succeeded, and it is debatable whether the field would ever have reached its current liveliness had he not found a disciple in Ray Harryhausen, his present-day equivalent.

Greater sophistication in both technique and audience reaction has not dimmed the energy of *King Kong*. It remains one of the most effective examples of pure entertainment ever produced by the cinema, a piece of brute action which steamrollers one's intellectual objections. Like the half-naked Fay Wray cuddled in the giant ape's hand, the audience is dragged bodily through the fights, disasters and final battle on top of the Empire State building without an opportunity to think or object. Technically, this is one of the finest examples of stop-action model animation ever produced. Kong's battles with the pterodactyl and giant snake are superbly organised, but O'Brien handles just as effectively the complexities of his attack on the native village, where Kong's fists crush huts and towers like egg-crates while fending off the spears flung at him. Max Steiner's relentless musical score, an eighty-piece extravaganza that is almost one sustained crescendo, aptly complements the images, especially those of Kong's island and the mist-shrouded cavern where much of the action occurs.

Unfortunately, *Son Of Kong*, despite the work of Steiner, O'Brien and Schoedsack, is unable to sustain the impact of its predecessor. The "little" Kong — barely twenty feet high — which Robert Armstrong discovers on a remote Malay island, is unremarkable after its gigantic ancestor, and the decision of Schoedsack to play it for laughs, giving the new creature rolling eyes and comical expression, dissipates the effect. O'Brien is on form with some competent natural disasters, but the finale, with "little" Kong standing underwater while holding above the waves his human master is too hilarious to be taken seriously. One might imagine that Schoedsack needed the steadying influence of Merian Cooper, the producer who conceived and co-directed *King Kong*, to make good films, but in *The Most Dangerous Game* (*The Hounds Of Zaroff*) (1932) and *Doctor Cyclops* (1940) he created two of the best excursions into the fantasy world yet engineered by an American. *Son Of Kong*, we must assume, is just one wrong step by a director who took very few during his career.

Despite the originality of *Dante's Inferno* and *King Kong*, fantasy cinema in America dealt primarily in the currency of other eras and areas. Even though the special effects of these films represented the beginning of a genuinely American fantasy cinema, reshuffling of Germanic and Gallic elements remained, as it does today, a simple method of producing commercial product. Periodically, the remakes and sequels transcended their material to remind us of the great glories of early Thirties horror films. One such film was *Son of Frankenstein* (1939), in which director Rowland V. Lee created an elegant variation on the old plot. Here is the monster (Karloff) again revivified by the son of Doctor Frankenstein (Basil Rathbone) and the distorted Igor (Bela Lugosi) whose head cants crazily to one side on an ill-mended broken neck. Set in and around Frankenstein's wrecked laboratory, with its seeping underground passages and ruined dome like a crushed skull, the action is fairly predictable, but enlivened by intelligent direction and lighting. The castle is no luxury chateau but a crumbling ruin with Caligari-like corridors whose walls lean into writhing perspectives. There is a sustained air of the grotesque, encouraged by effectively directed sequences such as that in which the monster lumbers into the bedroom of a child while outside a maid sits blissfully unaware, and a kind of sick humour in the presence of Lionel Atwill, a police chief with an artificial arm, the original having been torn off by the monster when he was a child. To smoke, he wedges the cigarette between black-gloved fingers and drags mechanically on it in a manner reminiscent of Peter Sellers's Dr. Strangelove twenty-five years later.

Another remake, but more elegantly contrived, was *The Cat And The Canary* (1939), Elliott Nugent's reworking for Paramount of Paul Leni's 1927 Universal masterpiece and first of a series of more or less inept adaptations. The Bob Hope-Paulette Goddard casting does not, surprisingly enough, detract from the atmosphere; it has, in fact, some of the panache of the old fantasy radio dramas like "The Shadow", "I Love A Mystery", and "Inner Sanctum". Bob Hope plays a radio comic, and his quips have just the right nervous quality. Nugent, a comedy director whose *Scared* (*Whistling In The Dark*) (1933), with Ernest Truex and Una Merkel, is a notable comedy-thriller, builds well to his atmosphere. The milieu is familiar — a rotting mansion in the middle of a swamp, sinister housekeeper (Gale Sondergaard), a group of frightened relatives who expire at regular intervals through the night, victims of a malevolent force. The drama, as in so many of these films, comes from the fact that the heroine must survive until morning to earn her inheritance; the twist is that the "monster" is one of the other relatives anxious to collect for himself. It is all familiar, but the old terror is still there.

Nugent's introduction of the house is effective; mist-wreathed gables, a glimpse caught of Sondergaard through a grimy window. The black cat which accompanies and sometimes seems to *be* her is a sinister symbol, used later by Nugent to introduce the "red-herring" menace, an escaped maniac who thinks he is a cat and creeps around on all fours. The point is hammered home by a brief shot among the most horrific in the cinema; the shadow of a crouching man thrown hugely on the wall, to dissolve into the shape of a cat, then vanish. The "real" monster which inhabits the passages under the house is a hideous creation, a gangling stalker in long robes whose stiff hulking walk is made all the more terrifying by its speed; pursuing Goddard along the cramped corridors in the final sequence, it moves at a maniac pace that is made by lighting and editing not funny but subtly horrible.

Familiar though the cards may be, Nugent has dealt them with notable skill.

In examining any area of fantasy film, it will always be the dealer's skill rather than the face value of the cards which is our yardstick. The Thirties in Hollywood saw elements of fantasy film from many countries, mainly Germany, adopted by Hollywood film-makers and adapted to their needs. The golems and vampires were, because they were unknown, approached with a fresh and inventive eye by the directors in charge of horror films. Later, the freshness wore off, that which had been new became cliché, while elements of the newly formed American style of fantasy, with its reliance on special effects and the literal depiction of the fantastic, began slowly to be incorporated in the body of work being produced. Today, we have a stew of styles and subjects, lumbering monsters and spaceships alternating in most films, the imagination of Whale and Freund largely dead and forgotten. It is hard to remember that the horror film was once the most coherent manifestation in American art of a tradition which had been old before that continent was discovered, and which brought the cinema to some of its rare peaks of pure creativity.

6. The Great Originals: 1

ALTHOUGH THE high average standard of Hollywood films during the Thirties is directly attributable to the studio system with its pools of talent and techniques, most of the period's major advances in cinema art can be traced to a group of independent directors whose unwillingness to work within the studio system gave them a greater degree of freedom than would have been possible otherwise. These directors seldom worked for the same studio on more than one or two films, nor did they approach in output the prolific studio men. They made at most ten or fifteen films each during the Thirties, many of them financial and artistic flops. Some were compromised by executives, some by the directors themselves. But the best of these are among the most important films that Hollywood has produced. These men, the great originals, worked out theories of film-making which have had far-reaching effects on world cinema. Because of their importance, other critics have already examined in detail their contribution to film; these chapters are intended only to pay tribute to their genius.

No theory of the cinema is tenable unless it accepts **JOSEF VON STERNBERG** as one of its major talents. Von Sternberg is more than a great director, a superb technician and an artist of genius; each of his films is an essay on visual theory in which is put forward his unique vision of art. To say his films are trivial is to miss the point, because von Sternberg has never viewed content as being of importance. "The best source for a film," he has said, "is an anecdote," and continued "Each picture *transliterates* a thousand words" [my italics]. His use of a word suggesting not the abandonment of script and dialogue but their metamorphosis into a visual form of expression provides the key to his work. Every shadow in von Sternberg's films has its meaning, every gesture and curl of smoke a relevance to character. The devices he employs to fill the "dead space" between camera and subject — nets, veils, smoke, shadows — are important as examples of a brilliant mind adapted to the necessities of film, but they serve as well a more subtle purpose, clothing his characters in the substance of a dream. It is impossible not to recognise a von Sternberg; at his peak, the works he produced were the greatest visual adventure cinema has afforded us.

Von Sternberg's best films are undoubtedly those he made with Marlene Dietrich — *The Blue Angel* and *Morocco* (1930), *Dishonored* (1931), *Shanghai Express* and *Blonde Venus* (1932), *The Scarlet Empress* (1934) and *The Devil Is A Woman* (1935). But even these vary sharply both one from another and within themselves. *The Blue Angel*, despite its characteristic aura and symbolism, is too heavily laden with plot to succeed completely. Lola Lola's song is still a great moment, the arrogant legs cocked over the chair, a sluttish swing of the hips, that feline stroll still Dietrich's trademark, but the school scenes with Emil Jannings and his silent-cinema acting style in general prove unequal to the load the director places on him. The praise of his final humiliation, paraded on stage in clown make-up to be mocked as a sexless buffoon, also seems misplaced, the embarrassed reaction of people who don't know what to make of it all.

One has no such reservations about *Morocco*, a film of impeccable balance and exquisite appearance in which von Sternberg's interest in anecdote is seen at its best. The affair between Gary Cooper's charming satyr of a foreign legionnaire and Dietrich's lost, sensitive cabaret singer is trivial, but the visuals sustain superbly the ambience of boredom and desire. Symbols of tropic exoticism predominate in von Sternberg's approach; a whore clasping a phallic pole surmounted by a skull, white burnouses flaring and blazing with slatted sunlight in the casbah, the fluttering fans of the café in which Dietrich sings, a symbol carried on cleverly to Cooper's appearance in her dressing room after the show, his hand reaching out automatically to a ledge from which, to his surprise, the fan placed there by Dietrich's predecessor (and, by implication, another of his mistresses) has been removed. But if the others had been unremarkable, the final sequence, of Dietrich interrupted at the dinner table by the sound of legionnaires returning from a skirmish, her nervous hands breaking a string of pearls, the frenzied run past shaded lamps and palms to her lover, and her resigned trek out into the desert with the rest of the camp-followers as the sighing wind comes up over the end title would alone have made this film impossible to forget.

Dishonored, *Shanghai Express* and *Blonde Venus* resemble each other so much that comparisons are impossible. All have their set pieces, their exotic Dietrich characters, but also their elements of the ridiculous, like Dietrich ecstatically playing the piano in the death cell in *Dishonored*, and her maundering devotion to dying husband Herbert Marshall in *Blonde Venus*. Of them all, *Shanghai Express* is undoubtedly the most remarkable, a film in which von Sternberg creates an entire universe to justify the actions of his star. The train, landscape and other characters serve no real purpose but to display and accentuate the character of Shanghai Lili. Everybody in the film is her creature; the fatalistic Anna May Wong, almost the spirit of oriental sexuality in a silk sheath that lingers on her slim body; Clive

Brook's stiff army officer, her love scene with whom on the observation platform is a poem of fur, smoke and husky whispers; the leering, foppish Warner Oland. None of them serve any good purpose except to show Dietrich at her best, yet the narcissistic tone of the famous shot where she leans back against a closed door and lets a cloud of cigarette smoke blaze up into the light, obscuring her face, indicates that it could not matter less to her what anybody thinks, does, says. Like another black-plumed lady thirty years later in *Last Year In Marienbad,* she might be part of another world, a world with only one inhabitant — herself.

No less ridiculous than the other von Sternberg films, *The Scarlet Empress* is of such visual bravura that criticism of its unlikely yet historically accurate plot is irrelevant. More than ever Dietrich is an object, to be displayed for her beauty rather than to move the audience or the other characters. The early scenes showing her childhood in Austria are a Greuze-soft *mélange* of garden picnics and family conclaves into which the message that she is to be absorbed by the Russian royal family intrudes, as does messenger John Lodge, "like a storm". Her suitability for the role of empress has been presaged in an incredible montage of torture, rape and mutilation, when she dreams of becoming the "hangman" of the Russian people, her fantasies culminating in a terrifying image of a huge bell in which the clapper is the body of a man. The destruction of her soft virginity by the violence of Russia is summed up perfectly in the instant when Lodge kisses his charge in the tavern where they stop one night, his black fur-swathed body obscuring, even devouring her with darkness. She is henceforth another of Russia's cursed ones.

Von Sternberg's Russia is like his China — false but ravishingly beautiful. Catherine's marriage in the candle-crammed cathedral becomes, characteristically, a study of the girl's emotions alone, the director closing in on her tremulous face to show, through a misting veil, her excited breath fluttering the candle flame in front of her. As for the rest, how can one sum it all up? There is no scene, no set or shot that is not an emotional experience. Sam Jaffe's spidering dwarf of a Grand Duke; the moment when a weaving auger wanders out of the eye of an ikon to provide a peephole into his wife's bedchamber; statues, twisted and contorted like Russia itself; huge lumbering doors which handmaidens labour to open and close; the secret staircase to Dietrich's apartment which her lovers climb to find her waiting naked for them in her veiled bed; an incredible finale with Dietrich in white hussar's uniform borne by her adoring troops through the castle like an arrogant conqueror. Von Sternberg has created in this film one of the cinema's supreme achievements.

For all his talent, von Sternberg was not a successful commercial film-maker, and his Dietrich films were in their way self-destroying. The late Thirties saw him left behind by an industry anxious for action and witticism, ruined by the same process that made Lubitsch's brittle comedy passé. His admittedly luscious *The Devil Is A Woman* was restricted because of political pressure from Spain and the low quality of the abysmal *Sergeant Madden* suggested that, deprived of Dietrich, he was incapable of making individual films. Only the fragments of *I Claudius* (1937), begun in England for Alexander Korda and closed down for a variety of reasons including Charles Laughton's intransigence, the cost and variable quality of the footage shot, have any hint of von Sternberg's greatness. Laughton is occasionally brilliant but one finds far more tantalising the scraps released of von Sternberg's shooting inside the huge columned halls of the Roman palace. The measured procession of white-robed figures which the BBC included in its film *The Epic That Never Was* far outdistances anything else shown, and it is alleged that at least one other scene in this set was filmed, viewed but never included in the TV documentary. The British National Film Archive holds most of the surviving *I Claudius* material, which includes some takes not included in *The Epic That Never Was*. Subsequent research, incidentally, makes even more suspect the documentary's implication that von Sternberg's autocratic manner with Charles Laughton was responsible for the film's collapse.

There are few directors who have made critical study of their films so difficult as has von Sternberg. Enigmatic, contradictory, evasive, his comments on direction are fascinating reading and worthless history.

He has dismissed the contribution to his films of scriptwriter Jules Furthman, cameraman Lee Garmes and set designer Hans Dreier, even though all three have left a clear signature on his films. His association with Dietrich is likewise confused, but while one would like to recognise the star's contribution, her continued insistence on his complete responsibility for her success makes such a concession impossible. The riddle of Josef von Sternberg will never be solved, but his films remain.

No two great directors of the Thirties differ so widely as Josef von Sternberg and **HOWARD HAWKS**. Von Sternberg would take a tiny situation and expand it to sustain an entire film; Hawks, on the other hand, could condense the First World War and three kinds of human tragedy into the space of ninety minutes and a single room. Von Sternberg's contribution to the cinema was in his visual theorising, his expansion of film language to convey subtleties which had previously been beyond it, while Hawks, less a stylist, showed that even the routine programme picture was capable of generalising seriously about relationships and society. One of the few American directors to leave an intellectual stamp on every major film he made, Hawks established the pattern of the *auteur* writer/director which persists today.

Hawks's respect for professionalism, and especially for the expertise of men who risk their lives for a living, comes out in all his best films, while the cameraderie of such men, and the love that can exist between comrades, male or female, seems to him to be the purest of human emotions. There is a halting statement of this belief in *A Girl In Every Port* (1928), but the first film to examine it in detail is also his first of the Thirties, *The Dawn Patrol* (1930), an Air Force story which stresses the man-devouring nature of war. Neil Hamilton, an American First War squadron leader bitterly hated by his officers because of the unit's high death rate, is replaced by his loudest critic (Richard Barthelmess), who then discovers the inevitability of the process for which he had blamed Hamilton. Soon it is his turn to be succeeded by the next in line, Douglas Fairbanks Jnr., and so it goes on.

However tragic Hawks may find the death of young men, he obviously feels the destruction of friendship by the pressures of war to be far more poignant. Unfortunately, the observation of character in *The Dawn Patrol* is carried on in dull set-ups and tedious dialogues which do not do justice to the situation. The film is only really alive in the air, when the splendidly photographed dogfights and air-raids, shot by Elmer Dyer, take over completely. There is a dazzlingly well-shot bombing raid, when two planes beat up a German base, swooping and diving with the agility of eagles, then add insult to injury by dropping the mocking gift of a pair of boots. A crash landing and rescue are also well photographed, with Hawks acting in a supervisory capacity and piloting the camera 'plane on more than one occasion. These scenes, re-used later in a number of films including Edmund Goulding's 1939 remake with Errol Flynn, are undoubtedly the film's main claim to immortality.

Hawks's most important film of the early Thirties was *Scarface: Shame Of A Nation* (1932), in which most of his preoccupations received their first genuinely competent and extended public expression. An effort to show Al Capone and his mob as a dynasty like the Borgias set down in Chicago, the film combines the talent of a great director with that of such key figures as producer Howard Hughes, scriptwriter Ben Hecht and cameraman Lee Garmes. Paul Muni (as Capone) is arrogant, vain and stupid, Ann Dvorak as his sluttish sister perfectly cast, George Raft suitably cool as the coin-flipping "Little Boy" whose romance with Dvorak leads finally to his murder by Muni, while Boris Karloff as mobster Gaffney and Karen Morley as Poppy, Muni's fluffy, intelligent mistress lead a superior supporting cast.

As in most Hawks films, the women in *Scarface* are either companions or camp-followers, and it is the conflict between these two roles in Dvorak's case that provides the film's main drama. Muni's incestuous love for his sister is clearly stated in scenes as explicit as any the cinema has seen, including one where Muni finds Dvorak kissing a man and throws him out. "You don't act like a brother," she rages at him. "More like . . .", and stops. Her affair with Muni's lieutenant Raft is ironic: Muni's two lovers go off together, leaving him alone. Only

93

in the end, when Dvorak returns to help him in his final fight with the police and dies in the resultant gun battle, does he seem to understand the enormity of what he has done to ruin his sister's life, and for this reason the gratuitously "moral" ending, with the quivering, terrified gangster mown down by contemptuous cops, seems irrelevant. In no other Hawks film has the death of a companion done less than ennoble the deprived one.

Visually, *Scarface* is superb, combining a Warners-like shadowy surface with intriguing symbols and set-pieces. Hawks uses, for no observable reason, the continuing symbol of a cross to indicate death. Karloff marks his bowls' scorecard with a cross a moment before he is murdered, a bowl leaving his dead hand to score a strike, the last pin teetering briefly before tumbling. The hotel room in which Raft and Dvorak are living is Number Ten — indicated on the door as X. And in the St. Valentine's Day massacre, the camera pans away from the execution to cross-shaped rafters above. The streamers of the opening sequence, where a cleaner shuffles through the debris of a mob party, sniffs a flower, but does not see a shadow whistling, accosting the party's guest of honour and shooting him coldly down, form just one of Hawks's devices to complicate and decorate the image. At the end, Muni stumbles around a tear-gas filled room lanced through with beams of light, and Dvorak vamps Raft at a night club by doing a sexy dance to a background of shimmering mirrors. Garmes is in top form, but it is Hecht's cynicism and Hawks's tough-minded attitude to personality that make *Scarface* so arresting.

Viva Villa! (1934), already examined under Jack Conway's career, was begun by Hawks, who worked, with Ben Hecht, on the script and also shot most of the interiors. It is generally agreed that Hawks directed about half the film, but it is difficult to allocate precise responsibility for the many remarkable sequences which combine footage Hawks obviously shot with that which he could not have. There is also more Ben Hecht than Hawks in *Twentieth Century* (1934), one of the earliest of the so-called "screwball" comedies which were to make Preston Sturges's reputation in the Forties. As producer Oscar Jaffe spending every moment of his trip on the Twentieth Century Limited talking star Lily Garland (Carole Lombard) into appearing in his next show, John Barrymore justifies in one role his immense reputation. Cajoling, demanding, even in one scene vamping the harassed Lombard, he projects a perfect image of Broadway panache and insanity. *Barbary Coast* (1935) has none of *Twentieth Century's* energy, although Miriam Hopkins as the girl who travels around Cape Horn to California to find her husband-to-be has been shot that day, gives one of her best performances. Joel McCrea as a poetry-quoting prospector is innocuous, but Edward G. Robinson in ringlets, gold earring, cheroot and ruffled shirt as the elegant Chamalis is visually if not intellectually arresting. The film, which Hawks does not especially like or remember, must be considered no more than a breathing space before his remarkable *The Road To Glory* (1936).

There are few films of the period which rise to the rank of tragedy, but *The Road To Glory* is one of them. Uniting two of the greatest actors of the period, Fredric March and Warner Baxter, and utilising the talents of Gregg Toland, William Faulkner and producer Darryl Zanuck, it is the most moving and accurate of all anti-war statements. Baxter's gradual decline as the aspirin-addicted commander collapsing from remorse and worry is a magnificently realised portrait of human suffering, added to by March's pitying lieutenant, soon to be chained, as was Richard Barthelmess in *The Dawn Patrol*, to the same treadmill of death. The strain of trench warfare has never been better conveyed than in the sequence where a terrified platoon lies quivering in the dark listening to German sappers placing explosives under their position, and its callousness is equally well rendered by their disinterested glances back as the group that has relieved them is blown up.

Hawks's interest in companionship rather than love motivates much of the script. A beautiful nurse (June Lang) comes each night from the hospital nearby to sit at Baxter's bedside and console him by her presence through his guilt-tortured nightmares, but sex is never mentioned. They are comrades. Her romance with March is something into which both are drawn against their will, and the remorse they feel at having betrayed their friend makes one doubt that the relationship will ever come to anything. The real preoccupations of everybody concerned emerge in the final scene, where March, taking over from the dead Baxter, repeats to the new recruits the same speech which his predecessor had made to each group of replacements. Love is all very well, Hawks says, but duty, professionalism and *esprit de corps* come first.

Taken off *Come and Get It* (1936) after a dispute with Samuel Goldwyn, Hawks may well have been glad to see the last few minutes of this disappointing production completed by William Wyler. Despite its splendid opening, with logging contractor Edward Arnold and his friend Walter Brennan demolishing a bar (and its patrons) with skimming metal trays which mow down everything breakable in sight, the film degenerates into yet another of the melancholy magnate dramas in which hefty Arnold repeatedly found himself cast after the success of *Diamond Jim* (A. Edward Sutherland, 1935). *Bringing Up Baby* (1938) is better, sustained by the maniacal energy of the affair between stodgy misogynistic scientist Cary Grant and Hawksian heroine Katharine Hepburn, but most of its humour derives, as did that in *Monkey Business* and other Hawks comedies, from dignity destroyed and romance satirised. For this reason, it is inferior to *Ball Of Fire*, a production in which these elements are worked out with a skill never attained in any Hawks film before or since. For all the popularity of his comedies, Hawks's reputation rests on the dramas (like *Only Angels Have Wings*) in which he revealed with an insight few directors have possessed the core of moral necessity which makes men more than intelligent animals.

There is an interesting polarity between the films of Howard Hawks and **LEWIS MILESTONE**, whose productions bear, in the matter of theme, many resemblances to those of the former. Milestone dealt, as did Hawks, with the importance of companionship. Many of his films have independent heroines and female characters noted for their toughness and male-like qualities. Yet, in mood, their films are widely separated. Milestone was interested, like Frank Capra, in social move-

The Thirties' most exquisite creation: Marlene Dietrich at right in BLONDE VENUS and below in THE SCARLET EMPRESS, both directed by Josef von Sternberg. The director is seen below right on the set of the ill-fated I CLAUDIUS with Merle Oberon and Charles Laughton.

Left, John Barrymore and Carole Lombard in Howard Hawks' TWENTIETH CENTURY. Right (top), Brian Donlevy, Miriam Hopkins and Edward G. Robinson in Hawks' BARBARY COAST; and (bottom), war as a destroyer of ideals: Lew Ayres comforts a dying comrade in Lewis Milestone's ALL QUIET ON THE WESTERN FRONT.

ments rather than people, and his characters are best viewed as representatives of universal attitudes, political creeds and social classes. Neither a consistent nor a commercial director, he nevertheless began his Thirties career on a high point, with one of the acknowledged classics of the American cinema.

All Quiet On The Western Front (1930) is still one of the most eloquent of anti-war documents, far outdistancing Vidor's *The Big Parade*, but it is as an examination of war in the social and cultural context that it is best remembered. Seeing the First World War from the German point of view, we are brought less to an understanding of war's universality than of its function as a social leveller and reviver for the flagging patriotism of complacent nations. The battle scenes, with their endless tracking shots and artfully designed soundtracks, such set-pieces as the nightmare of Lew Ayres trapped in a shell hole with the corpse of the man he has killed, and the famous last shot of the boy killed as he reaches for a butterfly (this last scene photographed by Karl Freund using Milestone's own hand, the rest of the film being shot by Arthur Edeson) are powerful indictments of war's brutality and pointlessness, but the details of recruiting, the continuing comments of the soldiers as they pass through a cycle of despair, rage, hope and despair again, and Ayres's visit to his old school where he makes a pacifist speech to an astonished group of students, both enlarge and diffuse the basic message.

The low-key nature of this film's incidents enhances its impact. Nothing could be more touching than the polite approach which the new recruits make to the old hands with whom they are billeted, while the brief interlude when a few of them swim the river at night to sleep with some French girls at a farm on the other side is the realisation of an adolescent dream perfectly appropriate to the film's theme. Trivial incidents such as the anger Ayres feels when more experienced soldiers calmly take the boots of his friend who has just died, and the visit to his mother back in Germany lend accuracy to Milestone's vision of war as a phenomenon in which men and nations are changed, not always for the best.

Unfortunately, Milestone did not live up to the promise of this first major film. *The Front Page* (1931), a newspaper comedy which contains some of Ben Hecht's and Charles MacArthur's best dialogue, did not entirely succeed despite a hard-driving style and competent acting by Pat O'Brien as a newspaperman and Adolphe Menjou as his cynical editor. Howard Hawks's remake (*His Girl Friday*, 1940) succeeded far better because of his skill with fast conversation and the Hawks-invented idea of making the reporter character a woman. *Rain* (1932), with Joan Crawford as Sadie Thompson and Walter Huston as the minister, was stiff and stagey. *Hallelujah, I'm A Bum* (1933), an attempt at a socially conscious depression musical which, despite rhymed dialogue, songs by Rodgers and Hart, and the acting of Al Jolson and Harry Langdon, seemed like half-baked Mamoulian. *The Captain Hates The Sea* (1934) gave us the sad picture of a declining John Gilbert, ulcer-ridden and alcoholic, lurching through his last screen appearance. *Paris In Spring* (1935) and *Anything Goes* (1936) were innocuous, but then, late in 1936, Milestone gave us a film which, for style and content, is one of the Thirties' undoubted masterpieces.

"They're refugees," an American explains as the Chinese pour past them down the crowded street. "They wouldn't pay their taxes. But General Yang fixed them. They understand pain well enough." His wife nods in agreement. Then a tall man with a marmoset on his shoulder steps from the crowd and asks the man for a light. "Sorry, I don't smoke." The tall man frowns and knocks him to the ground. "Refuse me a light, would you?" "I told you," the man expostulates, "I don't have a match." "And those people didn't have the pennies to pay General Yang," the tall man says. The marmoset twitters and he melts into the mob. This next-to-opening sequence sets both the scene and tone of *The General Died At Dawn*, just as it establishes in one quick sketch the character and preoccupations of Gary Cooper's O'Hara. A dedicated democrat working in China to foil the depredations of Fascist warlord Yang (Akim Tamiroff), he becomes involved with a woman (Madeleine Carroll) who, contrary to the pattern of such films, is neither tough nor ambitious, but a nervous, lost girl drawn against her will into a violent situation that terrifies and sickens her.

"I'm one of the nameless legion," Judy Perrie says, "that always gets stuck." Shackled, through pity and necessity, to a consumptive father (Porter Hall) whose one wish is to raise enough money to die in America, she accepts, reluctantly, the order of Yang to lure Cooper into a trap. Waiting in a train compartment for him to come by, she broods on her duplicity and flicks off the window-sill one by one the half-smoked cigarettes she has lined up there. But when Cooper arrives (a nice shot of the marmoset creeping through the half-open door, the camera tilting up to show his face and Carroll's reflected in the mirror. Carroll — "Boo") she is unable to resist his easy charm, and his implied appeal for help ("There are things on the ground that don't like me") moves her to respond to his advances until, as he bends to kiss her, she realises this is the man she is to send to his death, and her head twists away in pain, her face turned, as if from the light, down to the floor.

Madeleine Carroll's characterisation of Judy Perrie is perfectly realised. The thin pencilled eyebrows, tight turned-down mouth and blonde hair, its waves as smoothly rippled as brass, are vital parts of a complex and believable personality. Clifford Odets's lines for her reflect a life so full of bitterness that it is not too surprising she should offer it almost casually at the end in return for Cooper's. Her affair with him has the beauty of complete inevitability. "We could have made beautiful music together," Cooper says, "We could have made a circle of light and warmth," and the simple words seem to evoke just the world she wants, an uncomplicated place full of things others take for granted. The division of loyalties which her love for Cooper demands, her horror at the death of her father, shot of necessity by Cooper, lend to her character a sensitivity seldom found in the cinema.

In terms of cinematic invention, *The General Died At Dawn* is a fascinating technical exercise. Although Milestone considers the film of little consequence, having adapted it from a pulp magazine story to keep himself occupied between pictures, it shows, in addition to his interest in the problems of individuals trapped between opposing social forces, the breadth of his technique. Madeleine Carroll is introduced as the silent fourth partner in a billiard game, her head obscured in shadow until she bends forward expertly to play her shot. Bridging this scene and the next, Milestone engineers one of the most obvious but expert match cuts on record, dissolving from a billiard hall to a round white door knob, which then turns to take us into the bar next door. Later there is a four-way split screen effect, where, as somebody wonders how the four protagonists are progressing, we see their various situations displayed simultaneously on the screen. The finale, with Victor Milner's camera tracking sinuously through the Hans Dreier/Ernst Fegté Chinese junk sets, is a bravura piece of direction, providing a fitting finale to this, Milestone's most exquisite and exciting if not most meaningful examination of social friction in a human context.

The interest of **FRANK CAPRA** in society and its effects on individuals was far more perceptive and sweeping than that of Milestone, embodying an almost mystical belief in the ability of man to triumph over the social forces which threaten at every turn to crush him. His films celebrate the archetypal American hero, a barefoot boy with brains; slow, patriotic, shrewd as the Devil. Perhaps because of his frequent use of crowds to accentuate the brute force of the mob and the fragility of his heroes, he became adept at directing large groups of people, and in handling the complex editing techniques involved in illustrating dramatically the power of crowds, their movement and reactions. Always, however, his films show an inflexible faith in the power of the individual to prevail, and in the essential goodness of honest men.

Capra's early films — *Ladies Of Leisure* and *Rain Or Shine* (1930), *Dirigible* and *Miracle Woman* (1931) — do not exhibit to any degree the Capra style, but *Platinum Blonde* (1931) shows signs of an awakening interest in what was to become his major theme. Substantially a variation on the stock triangle drama, it has Jean Harlow as a spoiled socialite and short-lived but promising star Robert Williams as the newsman she steals from his tough fellow reporter Loretta Young. In a key scene, Williams, tired of affluence, invites Young and his old friends to visit him at the family mansion, the resulting party degenerating into a mocking assault on everything both Williams and Capra hate — sham, ostentation, the unearned superiority of the rich. Both in its handling of disorganised movement and in the bitter moralising of the script, this party sequence is the first to show Capra in form. Additionally, it marks one of his first collaborations with scenarist Robert Riskin, eventually to write for him on most of his major films.

The Bitter Tea Of General Yen (1933) has hints of Capra's preoccupations, with Barbara Stanwyck opposed to Nils Asther's warlord in a China reminiscent of *The General Died At Dawn*, while *Lady For A Day* (1933), remade in the Fifties as *A Pocketful Of Miracles*, is, despite its Runyonesque ambience, trite and clumsy. Capra's triumph however was *It Happened One Night* (1934) which swept up five Oscars and established itself as one of the Thirties' best remembered films. Cheaply made by Columbia with Paramount's Claudette Colbert and Metro's Clark Gable, loaned as a punishment, it is a smoothly realised exercise in the Capra specialty—falsity pricked, independence triumphant. Riskin's script is clever in a way which presages Sturges, Joseph Walker's photography luminous enough to glamorise even the bus stations and primitive motels where much of the action occurs.

Unfortunately, *It Happened One Night* does not retain today its topicality and charm. The premise, admittedly, is shrewdly developed; one cannot help but like Gable's rebellious newsman and the fugitive heiress (Colbert) whom he adopts during an inept attempt to make her way by bus across America. Though characterised, at least initially, as a snob, Colbert comes across as a nice, confused girl, resourceful in the best Capra tradition, so that their attempts to complete the journey become conventional exercises in frugality and the avoidance of authority. Much of the moralising is thin and obviously unfelt, so that the film's best sections almost always involve the tricks played by the couple on those who hunt them — Gable scaring off a noisy salesman (Roscoe Karns) with deadpan offers to give him a gun and let him in on the plan to "kidnap" Colbert, or the convincing domestic wrangle the couple stage for the benefit of suspicious police. Occasionally there are sequences which succeed on a level other than that of comedy, such as Colbert's brief moment listening to rain on the motel window before dropping off to sleep, and tracking shots down the crowded bus suggesting some of the *ennui* of the long journey, but in general the film competes to its cost with other more astringent comedies of the time.

Broadway Bill (1934), remade as *Riding High* in the Forties, is little more than a variation on *Platinum Blonde*, with Warner Baxter's recalcitrant racehorse owner finally turning his back on a rich fiancée and a business career to stay with racing and the independent girl he loves, but Capra followed it with what is still one of his best remembered films, *Mr. Deeds Goes To Town* (1936). Like *It Happened One Night*, this film does not wear well, but its structure is sound and as an exercise in the development by Capra of his favourite theme it is often successful. In the part of Longfellow Deeds, the tuba-playing country boy who inherits a fortune and is gobbled up by the city slickers, only to be revealed as yet another indigestible Capra hero, Gary Cooper is laconic and gangling enough to be a caricature of himself, but smooth direction keeps him integrated into the film's fabric.

The team of Riskin and Walker again gives the film a polished sense and surface. Cooper's assimilation into the world of the rich is cleverly handled, with the bewildered heir besieged by lawyers, tailors, servants, and the president of the New York Opera, all of them anxious to get their slice quickly, though not perhaps as anxious as the dead man's crooked attorney (Douglass Dumbrille) who must get hold of Cooper's money before the books are audited. Cooper proves, however, to be elusive. In the middle of a meeting of the Opera board, he runs to the window to watch fire engines, but returns to demand of an astonished group that they make opera pay or close the hall down. Wary of almost everybody, he does not suspect newswoman Jean Arthur, who shows him around town and surreptitiously lampoons him in her paper. Predictably, the film's second half is a Capra spectacular, beginning with scenes of Deeds's mansion bulging with anxious workers applying for some of the millions he is giving away to set up farms and so help an ailing economy. The courtroom scene is also splendidly handled, with the spectators surging into applause or protest at each new disclosure in the examination of Cooper's sanity. Perhaps everybody is a little too easily convinced, but the effect is consistent with the air of fantasy which Capra achieves in all his films.

Capra's three remaining films in the Thirties were *Lost Horizon* (1937), *You Can't Take It With You* (1938), and *Mr. Smith Goes To Washington* (1939). The last was another piece of self-plagiarism in which country innocent James Stewart defeats the political counterparts of the slickers Gary Cooper vanquished in *Mr. Deeds*, while *You Can't Take It With You* transposed to the screen Kaufman and Hart's Broadway success with little attempt at cinematic individuality. *Lost Horizon*, however, is surely one of the most impressive of all the Thirties films, a splendid fantasy which, physically and emotionally, lets out all the stops.

Opening in a London club with habitués speculating on the disappearance of explorer Ronald Colman, the film flashes back to the familiar setting of revolutionary China, though enlivened in this case by Capra's skilled handling of crowds. Struggling to board a 'plane, Colman and his party are buffeted and beaten by surging mobs of Chinese, and even when it is aloft their journey is an uncertain one, the aircraft jittering and lurching in a vertiginous evocation of primitive flying conditions. The group's discovery that its destination has been changed to Tibet comes as a shock, and there is an almost fevered intensity in the scenes where the 'plane lands to refuel on a vast windswept plateau, the passengers staring dazed at the lines of coolies dragging petrol cans, the grotesque faces pressed against the windows, the howling wind which seems about to sweep both humans and aircraft away.

By contrast, the hidden kingdom of Shangri-La to which they are taken is a haven of contentment and quiet, its smooth white walls, flower strewn paths and calm reflecting pools creating an aura of peace into which Colman sinks gladly. Forced however by the rest of the group to leave, he alone survives, and the last shot shows him struggling back across the mountain, an infinitesimal figure spidering up the sheer cliff in a biting storm, determined to reach again his paradise. Completely in control, Capra handles the novelettish story with the instinctive skill of a mystic, evoking the brute ferocity of high mountains and the savage storms which rack them in a way which even Fanck's pre-war films could not equal. The sense of an alien China, brutal, windswept, empty of all but the toughest of life, is also perfectly conveyed, contrasting effectively with the calm of Shangri-La. While perhaps not typical on the level of plot, *Lost Horizon* is true Capra; in its acceptance of individuality as the noblest force in man, in its drawing of society in terms of a mob from which only the strong of spirit extricate themselves it is perhaps his purest and most coherent statement.

7. The Great Originals: 2

THE LINE between genuine originality and mere artistic and technical competence is a difficult one to draw, and becomes especially elusive in the Thirties after one has left behind the handful of directors whose work is patently individual in form and content. Somewhere between the brilliant but studio-dominated films of Curtiz and Brown and the pioneering exercises of von Sternberg, there existed a world of the cinema in which great talents, operating erratically and sometimes without observable genius, produced work which was by turns mundane and advanced. These directors, almost without exception, began as studio hacks, progressed to confused but intermittently original work during the middle Thirties, then at the end of the decade and on into the Forties produced their greatest films. The seeds of their talent are apparent only occasionally in the Thirties, but a close examination of even their least remarkable films will occasionally reward one with a speck of gold.

The career of **JOHN FORD** is among the most vexed in cinema history, combining brilliant exercises in technique with plots which slip over into bathos at least once during their unravelling, but occasionally strike a note of pure and moving sentiment. Never able confidently to decide what sort of film he preferred to make, Ford's work has taken almost every form from rural comedy to symbolic drama. His interest in companionship between men, and especially brothers, has always been marked, but only a few of his films exhibit this pre-occupation. Unlike Hawks, he never adequately explored the theme, nor thought to extend it further than the level of occasionally effective sentimentality. Too often, he sacrifices a film with one hand and saves it with the other. It is only his skill as a technician and director of male actors that sustains his tangled career.

Throughout the Twenties and Thirties, Ford occupied himself as a staff director with the William Fox organisation, shifting to Columbia or more frequently RKO for less conventional productions. Initially, like William Wyler, a director of quickie action dramas, he earned some fame with *The Iron Horse* (1924) but did not capitalise on it, and his films of the early Thirties are largely sound versions of the type of production in which he was already expert. *Black Watch* (1929), his first all-sound film, is a British Indian Army story. Co-directed with David Butler, *Salute* (1929), a tame officer cadet story cli-maxed by an Army-Navy football game, was followed by *Men Without Women* (1930), a submarine story with a tautly written climax in which the crew is rescued at the last moment from the wrecked craft lying on the seabed. Clipped dialogue and atmo-spheric low-key photography effectively suggest the claustrophobia and tension, and Ford's direction is assured. The film was historic, in that it brought together for the first time Ford, cameraman Joseph August and scenarist Dudley Nichols, the team which was to make *The Informer* and other Ford successes.

After four miscellaneous comedy-dramas, including the curious *Up The River* (1930), with Spencer Tracy and Warren Hymer as a pair of headlong jailbreakers, Ford made *Arrowsmith* (1931), one of his most ambitious and successful dramas and the first to show the control of camera movement and actors which was to mark his Forties films. Sinclair Lewis had persuaded Samuel Goldwyn that his Nobel Prize winning novel would make a good film, but its episodic nature made adapatation difficult. Sidney Howard's script is however entirely successful, while Ford's direction and restrained acting from Ronald Colman as the idealistic Doctor Martin Arrowsmith and Helen Hayes as his wife Leora give an intensity to the film that few of its contemporaries attain. Condensed by Howard into the story of a young doctor struggling with public apathy and professional envy to pursue his calling in a small American city, *Arrowsmith* allows Ford to achieve splendid effects — the impersonal perfection of modern architecture dominating Colman, the soft focus shadowy death of his wife, the almost hallucinatory tension of an epidemic. A. E. Anson's clumsy Professor Gottlieb and Myrna Loy's Joyce Lanyon, the girl who falls in love with Colman but is rejected by him, lead a superior supporting cast which Ford handles with assurance. As literary adaptation and pertinent social comment, *Arrowsmith* is among the best films of its time.

Air Mail (1932) saw Ford returning to his old speciality, the action melodrama, this time a flying story about wisecracking Pat O'Brien humping mail over the Sierras. A wrestling drama with the inept Wallace Beery, *Flesh* (1932) is unremarkable, while *Doctor Bull* (1933) is a conventional film novelette of the period, though it starred Will Rogers in a rural role similar to that he would play later in *Judge Priest* (1934). *Pilgrimage* (1933) is clearly more than a novelette. This film of a mother's interference in the life of her son, and eventual redemption on a visit to his grave in France, comes from the heart of Ford's work. Aside from Boris Karloff's performance as a religious fanatic slowly deteriorating as the group of which he is a part stumbles around the Mesopotamian desert, *The Lost Patrol* (1934) is forgettable, though the quiet tenor of the playing is sometimes effective as a foil to the austere desert settings and the inevitability of the death which faces the party. As a result of the success of *The Lost Patrol*, Ford and Nichols were able to persuade RKO to make a film both wanted desperately to do and which Ford had been planning for five years. The result was his greatest success and the real beginning of his reputation.

However much one may object to Nichols's political emasculation of the Irish "troubles" and the stage-bound nature of the film's *mise en scène*, there can be no doubt that *The Informer* (1935) is one of Hollywood's great triumphs. Ford and August have transposed Liam O'Flaherty's novel with heightened fidelity to the screen, capturing the mood of Dublin and Gypo Nolan's brutish character in a way that the book never did. As Nolan, Victor McLaglen gives one of his few good film performances, a characterisation aided by Ford's careful direction. Lumbering along the street in one of the first shots, Gypo's head collides with a swinging sign, a device with which Ford establishes both his size and stupidity. His decision to turn in a friend to the Black and Tans in order to escape to America is consistent with his character, and the low lighting in the police station, emphasising the Neanderthal crudity of his skull, shows Ford and August working in complete accord to suggest the man's simple, even animalistic nature.

The foggy streets, Van Nest Polglase's shadowed sets and the way in which August sends beams of light lancing through the mist create a nightmare world where Gypo wanders in the dark, excluded from society by his guilt. The "Wanted" poster which pursues him as a silent accusation of betrayal, the frequent double exposure appearance of the dead IRA man, the blind beggar who taps after Gypo — all these are symbols which to a modern viewer seem tired and obvious. Far more effective and subtle are such shots as the first appearance of Gypo's lover (Margot Grahame), her shawl draped madonna-like around her head, then falling to reveal the hard, arrogant face of a whore. And although Nichols has cut from O'Flaherty's story the Communist overtones, Ireland's political chaos has never been more beautifully symbolised than in the scene where the police search a boy singing on a street corner to the accompaniment of a friend's scratchy violin. Still singing "The Minstrel Boy" he rotates once as the police check him for weapons, his upraised hand taking the coin one of them offers and then, in the same movement, flinging it contemptuously away.

After *The Informer* Ford's films underwent a noticeable change. Adventure stories were replaced by socially oriented dramas, many of them with historical themes, and when he returned to his old milieux it was with a heightened sense of their true nature and a technique which allowed him to extract from traditional themes values nobody has sensed in them before. Of the historicals, *The Prisoner of Shark Island* (1936) is largely conventional, despite a complex performance from Warner Baxter as Doctor Samuel Mudd, the country physician who treats the fugitive John Wilkes Booth and is sent for his pains to the penal colony of Shark Island in the Dry Tortugas. When Nunnally Johnson's script allows him to do so, Baxter holds the film together with an intense depiction of human indomitability and anguish, reminiscent in some ways of his role in *Forty Second Street*. The final epidemic is perfectly staged, Baxter slowly using up his inner resources until, in a convincing act of desperation, he fires the cannon which will bring in the fleet and save his patients. Unfortunately, such moving exercises in drama are neutralised by the obvious writing of other sequences, including that in which the decision is made by opportunistic politicians to proceed against Mudd, and the meeting between Mudd and Booth in the doctor's cottage. For all its drama, *The Prisoner Of Shark Island* is essentially a minor work.

Far more involved and challenging a film is *Mary of Scotland* (1936), in which an unpromising and stagey Maxwell Anderson play is fleshed out by the Ford/August/Nichols team into a rich and confident exercise in filmcraft. Without ignoring the melodrama inherent in the tragedy of Mary, Queen of Scots, Ford sketches boldly the complexities of the period in a way which, though focusing on the personal drama of the situation, makes the political and social implications readily understandable. As Bothwell, Mary's impetuous lover, Fredric March is arrogant and sardonic, adequately complementing Katharine Hepburn's occasionally spinsterish portrait of the Catholic pretender making her clumsy play for the throne of England. Florence Eldridge, hard-faced but convincing as Elizabeth I, and an elegant portrayal by the willowy John Carradine as Mary's Italian secretary and confidante, David Rizzio, are further props to Ford's re-creation of a confused period.

However, it is not so much the political tragedy in *Mary of Scotland* that is worth remembering as its remarkable visual expression of history. Ford shows us Scotland still feudal in thought and identity, a contrast to the subtler nature of England. There is a splendid polarity between the formal efficiency of Elizabeth's court and the raging arguments that stand in for government among the Scots, the lairds' baying hounds which compete with their masters for audibility, underlining the confused state of the nation. Ford too creates a memorable set-piece in the sermon of the patriarchal John Knox, an Eisensteinian figure in flowing robes and jutting beard who calls down hell-fire on the papist pretender, only to be drowned out by Bothwell's strutting pipers. Mary's trial by the English brings together the two elements in a brilliantly directed scene, enhanced by Van Nest Polglase's courtroom set, its bare floor and one lone chair overshadowed by a towering dais. The tragedy reaches its climax as the judges advise Mary that Elizabeth, whom she has never seen, has not attended the trial, but is present "symbolically". The single chair is indicated, the prisoner advised she can sit. "I prefer to stand", Mary says, "symbolically". The moment when, hearing of Bothwell's death, she moves quietly to this fatal chair and slumps into it, indicating her defeat, is perfectly realised.

The films which followed *Mary of Scotland* differ vastly from it in every regard. *The Plough and the Stars* (1937) is a halting adaptation of Sean O'Casey's play to which the Abbey Players add as little as Nichols's script. *Wee Willie Winkie* (1937) gave us Shirley Temple and Victor McLaglen in a production the sepia tinting of which was its main claim to immortality. *The Hurricane* (1937), while arresting in its sensuous re-creation of South Sea life and James Basevi's superb final storm with its Academy Award winning sound effects, offers little in plot and execution, while the most inept of the bunch, *Four Men And A Prayer* (1938), is a stiff-upper-lip melodrama of four brothers tracking down the murderer of their Indian Army officer father. Displaying all the chauvinism with which the Americans imagine the British are imbued, this is Ford's most painful production. "Cunning" ideas include such nicknames as "Snicklefritz" and an ending in Buckingham

Palace where the four heroes retire backwards from the royal presence to twitter about His graciousness. Except for hints of the brotherly love theme which Ford admires, there is little of him in this creaky farce.

During 1939, Ford released three of his greatest and best-known films. Of *Stagecoach*, it is necessary to say little. This has become the basic Western, a template for everything that followed. The often callous, always convincing picture of a dangerous coach trip across Indian country by a group of derelicts, outcasts and weaklings is as exciting in its depiction of character as it is in its Monument Valley settings and exhilarating action sequences. *Young Mister Lincoln*, as restrained as *Stagecoach* was brash, gives Henry Fonda his best early part as the young small-town lawyer exhibiting some of his altruism and determination in a court case long before his rise to President. Ford adapted this Lamar Trotti script with fidelity, but raised it to the level of film art with his careful illustration of rural life.

Drums Along The Mohawk again uses Henry Fonda in the role of a small-town man of honour, though the period is that of the Revolutionary War and the atmosphere far less tranquil. Ford's first film in colour, it re-creates with variable accuracy the beauty and terror of a war fought in the most beautiful of landscapes. Grotesquely painted Indians creep through the slanting golden light of morning or rage across peaceful fields to burn and pillage; British red-coats make mathematically precise patterns against the green of the forest. Otherwise the film is halting in visual style, Ford bringing the material to life only in the action sequences, the best of them that in which Fonda, running to get help for his besieged fort, is pursued by three Indians in a silent, almost stylised race for life. Occasionally there are subtleties; the death of the superannuated General Herkimer (Roger Imhof) who leads the ragged irregulars into battle, returns hunched up with a bullet in the stomach and dies in agony through the long night; Fonda's arrival at his primitive farm with new wife Claudette Colbert, the former embarrassed by its poverty, Colbert scared almost out of her wits by the appearance of her husband's towering Indian companion Blue Back, a creation worthy of a horror film. Perhaps Ford is not at his best in *Drums Along The Mohawk*, but in its combination of acute observation, over-humanistic direction of character and smooth visual style, it is a fitting end to his varied Thirties career.

While just as erratic a film-maker as Ford, **KING VIDOR** brought to his films an imagination and technical virtuosity which the former never attempted. Like Rouben Mamoulian, Vidor was bewitched by the possibilities of sound cinema, never tiring of experiment with new effects in the juxtaposition of sound and image, and in the use of non-realistic sound. Unfortunately he did not share with Mamoulian a sense of public taste. His deep involvement in his subject matter often led him into producing elegant tracts, but for all this his best films are among the most beautiful Hollywood has given us. Vidor's interest in the virtues of simple living and a natural response to life were presaged by *Wife Of The Centaur* (1925) and his masterpiece *The Crowd* (1928), but his first complete exploration of this theme was also his first film in the sound medium, *Hallelujah* (1929).

Coincidentally Rouben Mamoulian had also begun his experiments in the dramatic use of sound with an all-negro subject, in his case the Broadway version of *Porgy and Bess*. Both the subject matter of *Hallelujah* and Vidor's approach are obviously influenced by Mamoulian's vision of the negro as a simple creature dignified by his emotionalism and "natural sense of rhythm", but betrayed by a shiftless character, a tendency to laziness and excessive sentimentality. Although Vidor professed to have conceived the film as a picture of the "real negro", and backed this resolve by shooting much of it on location in the south under the most arduous conditions, the result is a false and specious portrait of negro life saved by Vidor's variable but often brilliant use of the medium.

Hallelujah's story of a negro preacher whose happiness is ruined by the theft of his wife and the rage which leads him to murder his rival makes little reference to the complex social situation which obtained in the south, preferring to dwell at length on picturesque incident and return to drama only at the climax, when the preacher pursues his quarry across a nightmare swamp to strangle him amid the alien

111

screeches of birds and the almost predatory sucking of quicksand. For the most part, however, *Hallelujah* and its inhabitants are mindlessly gay, the misery of decaying clapboard shacks and rutted streets neutralised by song and religion. The massed baptism, with its rows of swaying white-clad figures chanting a hymn of simple joy, the sexually charged night sequences, figures surging orgiastically toward one another to the moaning of a blues; all these are part of a view of negro life which, however much it may conflict with reality, has been imposed by Vidor on the subject with considerable skill.

Throughout his career, Vidor was often forced to make films which seemed to him trite and false. The tendency has been to discard these commercial films as untypical of him, but their quality is such that to do so is to ignore an important facet of Vidor's talent. Like many directors, he often worked best under control, and in *Billy The Kid* (1930) he struck a balance between the commercial necessities of Metro-Goldwyn-Mayer and his own vision of life. Some of the scenes were shot in 70mm. for use in the twelve theatres in the US fitted with the "Grandeur" system, and these allowed Vidor to experiment with the integration of character into landscape in a way never before permitted. In its gratuitous violence and sense of the West as an alien world where men make their own rules, *Billy The Kid* is the natural complement to Vidor's masterpiece, *Duel In The Sun*. As Billy, Johnny Mack Brown is brutal, violent but believable, Vidor building around him a landscape and society as bare and stark as the moon. Towns are dusty, run-down and austere; Billy hides out in a cave as big as a cathedral which suggests the implacability of nature in this environment. When death comes to people in the film it is brutal, agonising, without the subtlety of art. Billy's friend, going for water when they are besieged, staggers back shot in the stomach and dies screaming in pain. "I always was a whisky man myself . . . funny I should die for a drink of water . . ." Harsh and sadistic, *Billy The Kid* is a fit companion piece to *Scarface* and other exercises in the celebration of violent death.

Street Scene (1931), though remote in setting and theme from the brutality of *Billy The Kid*, further demonstrated Vidor's mastery in the

A perfect film: J. M. Kerrigan, Dudley Digges, Madeleine Carroll and Gary Cooper in Lewis Milestone's THE GENERAL DIED AT DAWN.

Frank Capra's idyllic Shangri La in LOST HORIZON.

Above (left), Frank Capra's most sweeping success, IT HAPPENED ONE NIGHT, with Clark Gable and Claudette Colbert; and (right), "I prefer to stand— symbolically": Van Nest Polglase's superb courtroom set perfectly complements Katharine Hepburn's performance as Mary, Queen of Scots, in John Ford's MARY OF SCOTLAND.

A drunken Gypo Nolan (Victor McLaglen) prepares to answer to The Party he has betrayed in John Ford's THE INFORMER.

Tom Keene (right) struggles to save the irrigation conduit he has laboured to build in King Vidor's socialist parable OUR DAILY BREAD.

One of the more skilled single-set stage adaptations: King Vidor's STREET SCENE.

The three (Joel McCrea, Merle Oberon and Miriam Hopkins) face their chief detractor in William Wyler's THESE THREE.

Director George Cukor, star Katharine Hepburn and cameraman Joseph August, on the set of SYLVIA SCARLETT.

Greta Garbo and Rex O'Malley in George Cukor's CAMILLE.

depiction of character as an extension of environment. Elmer Rice's play had analysed the conflicting emotions which can exist in a simple tenement building, and Samuel Goldwyn, pursuing as ever his goal of "cultural" films, saw no great barrier to adapting it to film. Vidor made use of a fluid camera to overcome the static nature of the action, craning dizzyingly to show the ant-like motion of people in the crowded street, tracking in and out of the carefully engineered sets to create the illusion of movement which the original lacked. As in *Hallelujah*, music supported and accentuated dramatically difficult scenes, occasionally getting out of hand but more often adding inestimably to the film's visual power. As a skilful adaptation of an impossible subject, *Street Scene* deserves comparison with Ford's *Arrowsmith* for its ingenuity.

However substantial the success of *Street Scene*, it was a film which Vidor had not especially admired nor involved himself with. Like those which followed it — *The Champ* (1931), *Bird Of Paradise* and *Cynara* (1932) — it exhibited a combination of technical skill and moral lassitude. *Our Daily Bread* (1934) is, however, one of Vidor's more personal works, financed by him but destined to see only limited release because of its controversial theme. At the moment when depression was fading from the world, it put forward the doubtful suggestion that co-operatives offered the best chance of economic stability for the United States. The director's intention to show the young couple of his silent success *The Crowd* joining with other unemployed to start a co-operative farm is carried out with a single-mindedness of purpose which ignores the political subtleties of the situation for a firm stand on the virtues of the human solution and of a return to earth and nature.

Our Daily Bread combines contradictory elements; the stars' acting is polished but much of the rest is indifferent. The scripting is often moving and literate, as in the scenes of discussion and consultation between the planners as they slowly pull together their concept of the co-operative, but crude to the point of melodrama in the foreclosure scenes and the depiction of official resistance to the venture. And although Vidor's camera is mobile and his use of sound well-controlled, the much-praised finale in which impressionistic techniques are used to show the triumphant building of the farm's irrigation channel has dated badly. While its sincerity is unquestioned, one cannot today accept *Our Daily Bread* as anything more than a well-mounted political tract from a theorist either unwilling or unable to see a situation with any real insight.

After the box-office failure of *Our Daily Bread*, Vidor returned to commercial film-making, and never again attained sufficient financial stature to produce a fully independent film. His skill matured, his control of the camera became even more assured while his halting experiments with sound came finally to an end, except for such bravura scenes as the gathering of McCanles's men in *Duel In The Sun*, with its chiming accompaniment of bells. His films of the late Thirties are unremarkable, marred by unimaginative subjects — Cronin's *The Citadel*, the old warhorse *Stella Dallas* — but distinguished by polished technique and direction of actors. Among the best of this period is the ambitious Goldwyn production which followed *Our Daily Bread, The Wedding Night* (1935).

Goldwyn never managed to launch Anna Sten as the new Garbo he has visualised her to be, and *The Wedding Night* was his last extravagant fling at doing so. Two million dollars were lavished on this intramural drama but, aside from Vidor's direction and variable work from Gary Cooper and cameraman Gregg Toland, it is unremarkable. One senses that Vidor was initially interested in the central conflict between a disenchanted New York author and the almost medieval family structure of a Polish immigrant community which prevents him from possessing the woman he loves. He observes the Polish customs with insight and a tacit approval of their simple virtues, even though this simplicity involves the subjugation of women, forced marriage and death for the one who transgresses. Cooper's nervous introduction to the family, the strained meal he eats with them and his growing love for the daughter (Anna Sten) are recorded with commendable detachment, while the orgiastic marriage ceremony, with its crude sexual innuendo, drunken carousing and Sten's violent death in a fall down the stairs is competently staged. Unfortunately the central conflict is never adequately realised, and one is left with the feeling that one has been cheated. As in so many of Vidor's films skill is vitiated by moralising, emotion by sentiment. Like Ford, King Vidor seems in retrospect to be a director who could have been great if only he had not tried so hard.

Diligent search among the films of **WILLIAM WYLER** for anything approaching a personal style has not revealed a great deal which might be called either individual or fresh, yet his films are among the most likeable, entertaining and deeply felt that the cinema has produced. Firm, competent, a great director of actors, Wyler is at his best adapting to the screen properties already devalued by use or intended primarily for alien media. Nobody was more professional in his transposition of stiff Thirties plays to the screen, nor better able to take a three-cornered one-room drama and expand it by pointed attention to detail into a moving personal statement.

Wyler's skill with interior drama was not foreshadowed by his early career when, as a director of two-reel westerns for Universal, he became expert in rendering the simple mechanics of the quickie action picture. The end of the Twenties saw him breaking out of the mould and although his first sound film *Hell's Heroes* (1929) is a Western based on the hallowed plot used by Ford and Boleslavski in *Three Godfathers* it has little in it of action melodrama. Shot on location in Death Valley, it is a harsh, brutal story of despair and endurance enlarged by Charles Bickford's acting, well controlled by Wyler in a way which indicates his gifted touch with male stars. Despite this promising beginning with an exterior subject, Wyler was next given a play to transpose. *The Storm* (1930), although an outdoor drama of a group of people snowbound in northern Canada, leaned heavily on dialogue for its effects, and Wyler's flair in handling the talky property encouraged Universal to give him more of the same.

The pattern persisted well into the middle Thirties, with Wyler's inventive adaptation of Elmer Rice's *Counsellor At Law* (1933) providing the single indication of originality. As the self-made lawyer driven almost to suicide by his unfaithful wife and saved only by the devotion of his secretary (Bebe Daniels), John Barrymore gives one of his most clear-headed performances. The single-set location of the play was an almost insurmountable barrier to real cinematic movement, but Wyler, by expanding the sets from one office to three and varying the action between them, managed to instil some flexibility into the static situations. Dated today in its dialogue, *Counsellor At Law* remains refreshingly clear in characterisation and agreeably well acted by a cast of seasoned professionals.

The Good Fairy and *The Gay Deception* (1935) were little more than conventional comedy-romances of the period, in sharp contrast to *These Three* (1936), a skilled adaptation by Wyler of Lillian Hellman's controversial play *The Children's Hour*. Samuel Goldwyn bought the play knowing that its lesbian theme would make it impossible to film with any fidelity, an understanding confirmed by the Hays Office which indicated that not even the title could be used in making the film. By replacing the original overt lesbian love of one girl for another with a straight triangle situation, Wyler feels that the original was hopelessly compromised, but although the dialogue states frequently that it is Joel McCrea whom Miriam Hopkins loves and not her companion Merle Oberon, the Hellman script implies at every turn that this love is based on jealousy and a wish to destroy that which has broken up the friends. Aside from a key confession of love for McCrea, delivered by Hopkins with her back to the camera, she acts throughout as if her desire was for her companion and not the man whom Oberon loves, the audience finding itself led inescapably to a conclusion at variance with the script but not with the mood and style of the film, nor the original play.

Whatever the film's motivation, Wyler's use of actors and Toland's camera build up a chilling atmosphere of suspicion, frustration and hatred. A slow track-in on the vicious Bonita Granville spying in the shadows suggests a world of malice and deception, while Wyler's idea in the final scenes of grouping the three friends always as a unit reinforces our image of them as still devoted to one another despite public

116

suspicion and contempt. His handling of the key interview with their chief assailant is almost stylised, the friends standing as stiff as statuary in poses which Toland shoots from low angles to emphasise their stability. Despite the compromises forced on him, this is one of Wyler's most integrated and formally perfect films.

Most of Wyler's major films for the next ten years were made under the auspices of Samuel Goldwyn, culminating in his perfect *The Best Years Of Our Lives*. Before this, however, Wyler directed *Dodsworth* (1936), a screen version of Sinclair Lewis's novel which, perhaps because of Sidney Howard's adaptation, bore an unhealthy resemblance to an earlier Howard/Lewis collaboration, John Ford's *Arrowsmith*. *Come And Get It* (1936) involved Wyler only to the extent of completing for Goldwyn the last few minutes of a film on which Howard Hawks had quit after an argument with the producer. *Dead End* (1937), by contrast, is one of Wyler's most famous stage transpositions, exhibiting, despite the director's dislike of its studio-bound atmosphere, a genuine originality of conception. Criticisms of its unreality seem beside the point when one considers the polemic fire Wyler was able to distil from the Sidney Kingsley original, assisted in its adaptation to the screen by Lillian Hellman.

Wyler's original intention was to shoot the film on location in New York's slums, but Goldwyn insisted instead on the use of a complex interior set which incorporates a seedy apartment building, a few shops, the rear entrance and balcony of a lush hotel and the designer's conception of a greasy East River backwater. Deriving much of its technique from Vidor's *Street Scene* but utilising as well the lighting genius of Gregg Toland, Wyler's style cranes easily through the narrow lanes with their artfully arranged garbage cans, peering down among the shadows, leaping back when action erupts, only to hover and drop slowly as in the death of Humphrey Bogart's Baby Face Martin to view the kill. One may legitimately question the acting of Sylvia Sidney and Joel McCrea, both as pure and unbelievable as the worst of Vidor's heroes, but Bogart and his delinquent auxiliary, the Dead End Kids, belong in this false and ugly world.

Equally false if less ugly, *Wuthering Heights* (1939) has become the

117

most highly rated of all Wyler's Thirties films, despite substantial defects in concept and execution. The film's pedigree is distinguished; if violence is to be done to Emily Brontë, by all means let it be committed by Wyler, Ben Hecht, Charles MacArthur, Gregg Toland and the arch despoiler, Samuel Goldwyn himself. This group, devoted to brining a windy, discursive and overheated original to the screen, has been less than gentle with its subject. Arbitrarily changing the period from Regency to Georgian in order to take advantage of the more picturesque costumes, Goldwyn went further and re-created an ersatz English moor on the hills of California, complete with acres of hot-house heather specially imported for the purpose. In the midst of this compromise and adaptation, it is not surprising that the atmosphere as well as the plot of the novel became obscured.

In the end it is the parts of Brontë's original concept which remain in this film that provide its most memorable moments. The romance of Heathcliff's love for Cathy does not survive without the fanatical intensity of the former's emotions which provides so much of the novel's power, and there is little of this almost divine anger in the film. Although he begins well, brooding in flashback like a malevolent despot over the crumbling ruin of Wuthering Heights, Laurence Olivier as Heathcliff loses most of his interest as Wyler leads him through a maundering romance with Merle Oberon's Cathy. Toland's lighting is admirably controlled but so soft and fragile that we lose all interest in a plot which demands melodrama if it is to be at all acceptable. The almost gothic horror of the early scenes, with Heathcliff driving his fist through a window-pane to grope for the ghostly hand of his dead lover that a visitor has felt clutch him out of the rain, should have been sustained and reinforced, but instead Wyler lets it fade into false romanticism. James Basevi's craggy designs for Wuthering Heights and the gloomy run-down interiors are effective, but unfortunately little happens in them that is worth remembering.

Estimates of **GEORGE CUKOR** as technician and innovator vary widely from critic to critic, some seeing him as one of the greatest of all artists, excelling as the director of female stars, others as a plodding hack saved by the competence of his actors. Neither view, however, seems acceptable as a summation of his talent, and even the most popular description of Cukor as "a woman's director" falls short of the truth. Cukor, in retrospect, seems a director very much of his time, responding to the stimuli of the moment with genuine insight, but finding his films left behind because of their very topicality while other more eccentric works have survived. His direction of women is competent, but his handling of male stars — John Barrymore in *A Bill Of Divorcement*, James Mason in *A Star Is Born* — is equally well judged. If his treatment of Garbo, Shearer and Crawford seems especially smooth, we must credit this to the fact that Metro, the studio for which he did much of his best work, excelled in its female stars. Cukor is a woman's director because the ritualised industry has typed him as such; his talents, while not as extensive as his supporters would have us believe, seem most notable in their flexibility and ability to adapt under stress.

George Cukor's introduction to Hollywood was anything but auspicious. A stage director imported to occupy the curious position of "dialogue director", a sort of voice coach/assistant director whose role decreased in importance as sound became better established, he essayed during the early Thirties a number of stage adaptations in which, allied with an established but usually untalented film director, he used his skill with actors, relying on his partner to sustain the visuals. The system was seldom successful, though in *The Royal Family Of Broadway* (1930), co-directed with Cyril Gardner, he managed to convey, mainly via Fredric March's energetic and thinly disguised parody of John Barrymore, some of the frantic verve of Broadway life. While the film's stage origins and Barrymore satire are obvious, Cukor's direction of March, Ina Claire as the disenchanted Ethel character and Henrietta Crossman as the *grande dame* who expires during a performance, forcing Claire to go on in her place and perpetuate the family tradition, is completely professional. One cannot help thinking, however, that there is a certain malicious relish in the way March, in his first film part, delivers the Edna Ferber/George Kaufman lines denouncing the myth of Hollywood. Perhaps Cukor's own views are summed up in Crossman's comment while driving along Broadway after a show. Glancing up at a huge poster of a bare-chested, madly grimacing March advertising his latest film, she sighs to Claire, "Oh dear — all action, all talking, all terrible."

Cukor's misadventures in co-direction came to a head in 1932 when, after beginning the Jeanette MacDonald/Maurice Chevalier musical *One Hour With You*, he was sacked by Lubitsch following disagreements over handling. The result, one must admit, is better for Lubitsch's contribution, so obviously appropriate is the subject to his style. After this debacle, Cukor transferred to RKO/Pathé, for whom he worked on his next four films. His first for them was the rare *What Price Hollywood?* (1932), a witty and biting parody of the film colony which parallels in some ways Wellman's *A Star Is Born* and Cukor's Fifties remake, the latter arguably his greatest film. As the waitress who rises to fame with the assistance of an alcoholic director (Lowell Sherman), Constance Bennett is engagingly tough and unsentimental. Although the ending descends to melodrama, Cukor's assured handling of the crisp Adela Rogers St. John dialogue gives the film a uniformity rare among RKO productions of the period. Emboldened by this success, Cukor created in 1932 one of his greatest dramas, *A Bill Of Divorcement*.

Although it seldom rises above its stage origins, *A Bill Of Divorcement* remains fresh today purely on the basis of John Barrymore's perfect performance as the amiably deranged father who escapes from an asylum on the eve of his wife's remarriage, forcing his daughter in a doubtful excess of filial love and duty to cancel her wedding and devote her life to his welfare. Despite their physical aptitude to the parts they play, Katharine Hepburn, Billie Burke and David Manners are little more than stage furniture. It is Barrymore, frightened, vague and lost, who totally dominates our attention.

Barrymore's unremarkable figure and sensitive face suit him physically for the role, but the adoption of a stoop, rumpled clothes, and a vague expression and tone of voice add dimension. He acts for the most part with complete conviction, speaking fearfully of "that place" where they locked him up, obeying instantly any order given him, then rebelling against it when he realises he is no longer under guard. The insane outbursts of religious frenzy when he raves about the face of God being turned from him are balanced by moments of great tenderness, especially when he allows Burke to go away with her husband-to-be rather than spoil her happiness. He is at his most pathetic in the brief flashes of lucidity, as when he frantically prepares to see Burke for the first time since his escape, examining his appearance in the mirror and begging his daughter, "Give me a minute, give me a minute . . ." Cukor seldom did better work, or used such substantial talent.

Dinner At Eight (1933), made at Metro, soon to become Cukor's primary studio, saw him again working with Ferber/Kaufman dialogue, and continuing his association with producer David Selznick who, when he switched from RKO, invited Cukor to join him. Exhilarated by the fabulous Metro machine, Cukor created in *Dinner At Eight* one of his most polished films, given an added gloss and style by Cedric Gibbons's shimmering white décor and William Daniels's high-key camera. Revolving around a dinner party thrown by the social-climbing Billie Burke, Cukor's film exposes in a series of cynically observed vignettes the unease and deception underlying urban high life. One by one the invitees are introduced; Marie Dressler as a decaying *grande dame* of the stage, Wallace Beery and Jean Harlow as vulgar magnate and sluttish wife, John Barrymore the destitute matinée idol who, finally deciding to put an end to his misery, turns on the gas in the hotel suite he can no longer afford and, settling back in his chair, narcissistically places the lamp so as to let its light illuminate his classic profile. With revealing and pitiless technique, Cukor cuts deeply into the decay of his time in a way that is both atypical and timeless, making this one of his most durable films.

Despite the topicality of *Dinner At Eight*, Cukor then found himself involved in a series of productions in which modern modes were abandoned in favour of literary adaptations little different in tone from his film stage plays but informed by a vastly matured style and sense of design. *Little Women* (1933), with its flawless Hobe Erwin design and competent performance from Katharine Hepburn, is still a watchable if slightly saccharine romance saved from tedium by Cukor's careful delineation of character and a sense of actor movement so strong that we never become confused despite the crowded dialogue sequences. *David Copperfield* (1935) is a similar triumph of control, though marred by the tendency on the part of design and writing staff alike to snatch points of Dickensian detail wherever they are offered. There is something relentless about the encapsulation of Dickens's sprawling narrative which impairs its credibility as David Lean's adaptation of *Great Expectations* never did. While credit must be given to Basil Rathbone's sinister Murdstone and W. C. Fields's Micawber, the performance of Freddie Bartholomew as David remains easily the most shrill and artificial this actor ever produced. Visually splendid, indifferently acted, *David Copperfield* is an interesting failure.

Cukor likewise fell victim to his material in *Romeo And Juliet* (1936), an extravagant rendering of Shakespeare in which Irving Thalberg, straining after reputability, cast his wife Norma Shearer and a mature Leslie Howard as the star-crossed lovers. Grossly overblown in its acting and saved only by occasional examples of control on the part of Howard and John Barrymore's Mercutio, there is little in *Romeo And Juliet* worth remembering, except perhaps its excess in every category from design to Herbert Stothart's typically clumsy pastiche of Tchaikovsky which stands in for a music score.

It is significant that Cukor followed this clumsy farce with one of his more delicate and controlled films, *Camille* (1937). Released from Clarence Brown's tight and sometimes parsimonious style, Garbo expands visibly as Marguerite Gauthier's tragic heroine, languishing with carefully judged negligence through her affair with Robert Taylor's almost excessively willowy Armand. Cukor, with the help of Gibbons's unusually frilly sets and the combined talents of Karl Freund and William Daniels on camera, gives Garbo a soft image she has never before attained, and while her performance seldom suggests a high-class whore whose imminent death from tuberculosis encourages her to a last desperate flutter of coquetry, it remains in its cool delicacy of approach one of her best.

Cukor's unfortunate experiences with *Gone With The Wind* (1939) effectively completed his Thirties career. *Zaza* and *The Women* (both 1939) belong more to the Forties, with their wisecracking humour and indelicate lack of charm. The gloom of his early Forties material did not lift until the cold polish of *Keeper Of The Flame* and *Gaslight*, and despite an always confident and professional style it is not until the early Fifties that we see Cukor again at his best.

Like Vidor, Wyler and Ford, Cukor frequently found himself betrayed by his material. All four lacked the sweeping social vision of their more individual contemporaries, and in attempting to make up for this deficiency by the extensive exercise of craftsmanship they lost touch with their subject or accepted for the sake of expediency properties suited neither to the cinema nor to their attitude. All might have been great if only they had remained as ruthless as the tightly controlled Curtiz, Brown and LeRoy. Yet, if they had, opportunities would not have existed for the leisurely schedules and expensive stars each needed to succeed. The paradox is as absurd as it is tragic.

8. Powers

AS HOLLYWOOD widened its scope during the early 1920s, it acquired by adoption the techniques and skilled personnel which, because of its brief history, it had been unable to develop within itself. The organisational systems of film management, the structure of the studio, producer/writer relationships — all these were products of Hollywood ingenuity. In aspects of entertainment already perfected elsewhere, however, the impatient studios tended to purchase the best available rather than grow their own. Actors, writers and designers especially came almost always from the theatre, as did a number of major directors, and it is for this reason that much of Hollywood's output in the years 1925-1933 is static in all but its technical aspects. It is only after the last problems of sound had been solved and the American cinema placed on a completely solvent basis that the techniques which we recognise today as exclusively those of film were perfected.

Despite the extensive borrowing from other fields, there were in Hollywood during the Thirties a number of executives, technicians and actors whose work showed an instinctive understanding of cinema and its requirements. These people, eschewing the traditions of the stage, worked to create the beginnings of a genuinely modern and national cinema, applying their intelligence to formulating new techniques and lines of approach. Frequently their work was hampered and reversed by others who lacked their skill, but even where the films themselves are lost their influence is present in the work of others who saw and understood. Many of these people are almost forgotten today, but their vision of the cinema lives on in its traditions and techniques.

The role of a producer is a difficult one to define. On some levels, it means somebody who finds the money and pays the bills. On another, his creative contribution to a film can be as important as that of the director. In general, the two aspects, commercial and artistic, of film production are widely separated, though it was in Hollywood during the Thirties that the techniques of creative production were worked out. There had been producers like this in European cinema — Erich Pommer, Alexander Korda — but they were rare. Hollywood was the first film producing complex to bring together the apparently conflicting considerations of art and money in a standard working arrangement.

IRVING THALBERG is considered to be one of the key figures in Hollywood in the Thirties. Studio manager of Universal at 21, production manager of Metro until his death in 1936, aged 37, he was responsible for the growth of Metro prestige and its establishment as the most "respectable" of the studios. Although often wrong in his estimate of future trends — he felt sound cinema would never catch on, took longer than most people to see that the stage was a poor source of cinematic material — his organisational and directorial ability were substantial. His name appears as producer on only a few films — The Marx Brothers' *A Night At The Opera*, Cukor's *Romeo And Juliet* — but as story and cutting consultant, script revisionist and general inspirational force his contribution to scores of Metro films is indisputable. The films he made with his own Metro unit, however, and the productions in which he had particular faith — Boleslavski's *Rasputin And The Empress*, *Romeo And Juliet* — were seldom especially distinguished and did not always make money, mainly because of their strong literary bias and self-conscious striving for "culture". In the end, Thalberg is best remembered as the gearbox between the powerful but philistine Louis B. Mayer and the more talented of Metro's directing team.

While Thalberg was devoted to the studio system and specifically to Metro, **DAVID O. SELZNICK** seldom stayed with one organisation for long. When he joined Metro as vice-president in charge of his own production unit in 1933, he had already had executive status in most of the big studios, and when he left in 1935 to form his own company was destined to continue as a major force through the late Thirties and Forties. A strong creative artist, he had more sense of genuine artistic quality than Thalberg, as witnessed by his productions. *Dinner At Eight* (by Cukor, whom he brought to Metro from RKO), *Viva Villa!*, *David Copperfield*, *A Tale Of Two Cities*, and *Anna Karenina* are all superior exercises in filmic creation, quite apart from their commercial success. Under the imprint of Selznick International, he produced Wellman's *A Star Is Born* and *Nothing Sacred*, as well as *Gone With The Wind* (see Chapter 2), following it in the Forties with such masterpieces as *Portrait Of Jennie*, *Rebecca* and *Duel In The Sun*. The Selznick motto "In a tradition of quality" is not without meaning; although he was often guilty of interfering excessively in the films he produced — the Powell/Pressburger *Gone To Earth* is a glaring example — their general quality was high, and there were few who could look back on so substantial a list of genuinely creative and cinematically important productions.

Lindsay Anderson called him "a great showman" and probably no other estimate of the role of **SAMUEL GOLDWYN** in the cinema is more accurate. Totally independent, owing allegiance to no studio, board of directors or any authority except the box office, he created through his career a notable string of variable and often brilliant films, from the most vulgar and garish of musicals (*Palmy Days*) to the zenith of social comment (*The Best Years Of Our Lives*). His most important work in the Thirties was that in association with William Wyler, most of whose best films were made under his banner. During the decade, Goldwyn provided Gregg Toland with the financial security to make his early experiments in film lighting, imported Busby Berkeley from Broadway and, less auspiciously, Anna Sten from Europe. He had many successes, made many mistakes, but the experience he gained from both was passed on to later producers who benefited from it. His greatest importance to the cinema is in the precedent he set for the genuinely independent non-artistic producer, a man who, though not himself creative, could create a climate for others who were. Once he had said it could be done and showed how, the way was open for a hundred others to break away from the rigid studio mould.

There is hardly an American screen actor of the Thirties who is worth considering in any objective rating of dramatic ability, so devoted are they all to the techniques of stylised, voice-oriented acting beloved of the late Twenties stage. During the Thirties, many actors and actresses made their debuts who, later in the decade and in the Forties, would form the basis of the first genuine school of cinema acting, but few of them came to prominence during the Thirties. Those people praised for their acting ability depended almost entirely for their effects on the technicians who presented them; Garbo was a presence, not a person — the same may be said of most stars of the period. A few actors and actresses did, however, reach peaks of dramatic ability which their later distinguished careers have indicated to be early signs of a great natural talent. Two of these (chosen, it must be admitted, out of personal preference, but from a very short list indeed) are Bette Davis and Fredric March.

In other chapters, both Davis and March have been considered in connection with specific projects. It is rewarding, however, to take a more general look at the qualities which contributed to their impact. **FREDRIC MARCH** is an actor worth studying as one who grasped with both an intellectual and intuitive skill the necessities of sound cinema. Formal in some early films, and inclined, as he did in *My Sin* (1931) with Tallulah Bankhead, to pose rather than perform, he became in a few years the most adaptable of all stars, a process in which he was aided by Warners' multiplicity of subjects. The ersatz John Barrymore roles into which he was forced because of the strong facial resemblance soon disappeared when his sardonic delivery became settled. In *The Royal Family Of Broadway* (qv), re-creating a role he had played on Broadway, he guyed superbly the whole star mystique, playing a character patterned on Barrymore as a combination of rake and clown, tolerated by an amused and affectionate family. The whirlwind entry into his mother's house, a fencing match up and down the stairs, the glassy-eyed and frenzied progress in which there was no time to think satirised and exposed for ever the empty myth of The Great Profile.

March's special ability was, and still is, to suggest genuine mental pain. As a portrayer of tortured and distressed men, he has no equal. The complete physical control which allows him convincingly to sag, stoop and collapse is assisted by a face suggesting at the same time both intelligence and sensitivity. His eyebrows are especially mobile, quirking at will into questions, statements of doubt or of cynical understanding, and he has no master in the art of the disenchanted and rueful smile. He seldom concedes to his fellow players the right to do more than respond to his performance, so that many of his best lines are delivered into the air, our attention being focused of necessity on his face and not on those to whom he is speaking. His is a talent of small touches which combine and resonate to create the pattern of a performance, and it is in this apprehension of the vital nature of minutiae to a screen actor that his genius lies. No one understands better than he that madness is in no way better indicated than by an almost imperceptible tic, that a quick and subtle smile can suggest more than all the talk in the world.

As in the case of March it was **BETTE DAVIS's** special forte to suggest sensitivity and pain, though both the nature and content of her performances were substantially different. Less mobile in her expressions and condemned by Warners in the Thirties to parts allowing little opportunity for the off-beat characterisations March was able to achieve, she relied for her effects on an essentially physical approach in which she used her arms and head rather than her face to achieve the necessary dramatic emphasis. No movements are more typical than the delicate gesture of a forearm, a brave lift of the chin. In her early parts as a fluffy blonde, perennially cast as gun-moll or shop-girl, or the later more mature characterisations of which her Joyce Heath in *Dangerous* and Judith Traherne in *Dark Victory* are the peaks, she projected, by the combination of girlish vulnerability and urban *sang froid,* the image of a bruised, sensitive woman gamely accepting life's adversities.

Although she feels her Academy Award for *Dangerous* (1935) was a "consolation prize" for having missed out the previous year with the much-overrated *Of Human Bondage*, the quality of her performance as the "jinxed" actress restored to greatness by adoring architect Franchot Tone is so well-judged that this writer has no such reservations. Here is an incomparable portrayal of human desolation moderating to hope and triumph. Initially morose, crushed, slumped over a drink in a dingy bar, she exudes despondency and an almost suicidal despair. Her revival at Tone's country house is a process we can see reflected visibly in her manner and voice, sustained by a perfect low-key sequence where she improvises a reasoned demand for Tone's disassociation from her while claiming to be reading it from a book in her hand. The peak of her performance is, however, a brief scene in which, to escape a storm, she and Tone run to a barn stacked with bales of hay. Rain and lightning enhancing the aphrodisiac effect of their exertion, the couple face each other in the damp, electrically charged air. Davis moves her arms in a

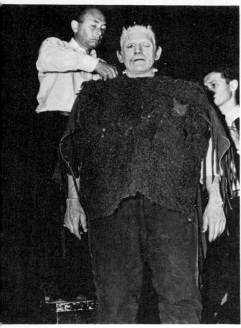

*ft, Boris Karloff is
ade up as the monster for
ON OF
RANKENSTEIN;
d right, "an actor who
asped with both an
tellectual and an
tuitive skill the
cessities of the sound
nema": Fredric March
Mervyn LeRoy's
NTHONY ADVERSE.*

*The genius of William
Cameron Menzies: a
set from his futuristic
fantasy, THINGS TO
COME.*

Performers integrated with settings: the set-up used by Busby Berkeley to achieve the staggering finale of FORTY SECOND STREET.

Carl Brisson and Kitty Carlisle in Mitchell Leisen's MURDER AT THE VANITIES

gesture of seductive negligence, offers a mockingly companionable half-smile, and we understand immediately the combination of sexual desire and malicious contempt for men that is both her mood at the moment and the key to her entire life. Epiphanies are rare in the cinema, and it is to the Davis genius alone that we owe this brief insight into the complexities of human behaviour. Hers is a talent beyond comparison, and nowhere is it more advantageously displayed than in her films of the Thirties.

Although Hollywood boasted the most distinguished collection of technicians ever assembled in any film-making area, the conditions under which they were employed did not encourage them either to experiment or transfer their attention to other aspects of production. The power which the more important cameramen, set designers and editors had over the films on which they worked was for most of them satisfaction enough, and to this we may attribute the high average quality of Hollywood films in the middle Thirties as well as its absence of peaks and audacious variations. However, despite this tendency towards stasis, Hollywood did produce its share of creative technicians whose occasional essays into direction and production indicate a desire to put the mark of their personality more obviously on their films. It is from these people, who added to the substantial body of technical knowledge the fire of a genuinely individual talent, that most of the major advances in film-making technique sprang.

At no time during his long career did **WILLIAM CAMERON MENZIES** achieve on any film a credit which adequately conveyed the nature of his contribution. Variously described as "Art director", "Production designer", "Co-director", and "Associate producer", his role appears to have varied from that of a conventional art director to full directorial control. Perhaps the now familiar *"metteur en scène"* comes closest to summing up his particular domination of the visual nature of all the films on which he worked.

Menzies's signature is apparent on a number of films in the Thirties, notably *The Adventures of Tom Sawyer* (Norman Taurog) (1938), *Gone*

129

With The Wind (qv) and his own *Things To Come* (1936), which he directed for Alexander Korda in Britain. The latter is one of the most perfect examples of cohesive visual organisation ever seen in the cinema, every detail from the entranced movements of the "Wandering sickness" to the overpowering magnitude of the future London sets contributing to a compelling vision of human history. *The Adventures Of Tom Sawyer* lacks the sweep of *Things To Come*, but it is faultless in its evocation of rural life in the age of American innocence. A calculated arrangement of tree limbs by the river, masterly colour contrast in the scene where Tom whitewashes a fence, the much discussed control of light in the cave sequence in which illumination leaks slowly into the image as the children's eyes become used to the dark and they sense the presence of another exit; all these must be credited to Menzies's genius. Although not absolved from the possibility of failure — his design for *Alice In Wonderland* is abominable — this artist's work exhibits a consistency of vision which must place him among the greatest talents of the cinema.

BEN HECHT had the misfortune to be expert in a branch of the cinema for which Hollywood in the Thirties offered little scope. Scriptwriting, as S. J. Perelman summed up, "is no worse than playing piano in a call house", and Hecht, failed playwright and footloose newsman, soon discovered the truth of this observation. He never ceased, however, to espouse causes and fighting in his own way for more truth in the cinema, even though his method was often to mock both his material and his audience. William Wellman's otherwise unremarkable *Nothing Sacred* (1937) is Hecht's cynical testament, with its opening title summing up all his disenchantment: "New York, skyscraper champion of the world, where the slickers and know-it-alls peddle gold bricks to each other, and truth, crushed to earth, rises more phony than a glass eye."

Hecht's was a genius which could be turned on to order. Not above handing work to friends to be "roughed out", he was nevertheless able to mark all his scripts with his particular combination of technical polish and wisecracking humour. Lubitsch's *Design For Living*, Conway's *Viva Villa!*, Hawks's *Twentieth Century* and *Barbary Coast*, Wyler's *Wuthering Heights*, Milestone's *Hallelujah, I'm A Bum!*: all have the Hecht sign on them. Typically, his films as director and producer vary in worth, often leaning towards heavy condemnations of social evil. *Crime Without Passion* (1934) and *The Scoundrel* (1935) have a melodramatic sweep and some of the cynicism found in Hecht's scripts, but the overall ambience is of engagement with causes long lost. Neither sensitive enough to be a great novelist nor tough enough to be happy writing scripts, Ben Hecht was one of the sadder Hollywood casualties.

There is no evidence that **BUSBY BERKELEY** had any such difficulty in adapting to the exigencies of Hollywood. His work as a dance director exhibits the cheerful eroticism which distinguished the best Hollywood comedy, unalloyed with the subtlety which Europeans like Lubitsch injected into it. Berkeley had no qualms about appealing to the lowest instincts of the American male, offering him the most obvious sort of calendar sex without any concessions to "taste". People have described Berkeley's work as "vulgar"; the adjective is ill-chosen. Vulgarity implies some variation from an accepted norm, an imbalance or distortion, but the Berkeley dance spectaculars had no such eccentricity. They were true only to themselves and to their own internal logic. Conceived and directed entirely separate from the films in which they appeared, these dances merit consideration on their own.

Brought to Hollywood in 1930 by Goldwyn, Berkeley had a substantial reputation as a director of stage shows, but his work in such early films as *Whoopee* (1930) and *Palmy Days* (1931) is undistinguished. In both, he depended on routines borrowed from the stage, consisting mostly of a chorus line facing the audience in single file or straight line and performing simple tricks designed to show off their legs. A long tracking shot during the "Bend Down, Sister" number in *Palmy Days* presents us with the cleavage of each Goldwyn Girl in turn as she bends to the inquisitive camera, while later sequences obviously duplicate stage effects. It was not until he went to Warner Brothers and gained the use of that studio's technical expertise that he began to

131

produce his most remarkable work.

Forty Second Street, Berkeley's first Warners film, is in many ways an apprentice work, without the flair of later productions. "Young and Healthy" is sung by Dick Powell surrounded by fur-enveloped chorus girls, but it is the song's gaiety that makes it memorable, while "Shuffle Off To Buffalo" offers us, aside from the surprise of a jack-knifing train carriage, little but the sly sexual lyrics of the Warren/Dublin song. Only the title finale, with its hints of the "story-telling" technique which Berkeley was to use later with more skill, is genuinely creative. Massed tap-dancing whores and criminals, a mobile craning and tracking camera, and the final dolly in to Powell standing at a bar and commenting "The big parade goes on for years/A melody of laughter and tears" make this one of the better Berkeley extravaganzas.

From this point on, there is a growing disparity between the more conventional songs and those which Berkeley saw as having story potential. "We're In The Money" and "Shadow Waltz" in *Gold Diggers Of 1933* are more or less thrown away, but the much discussed "Pettin' In The Park" gets the full treatment. Powell and Keeler are in raffish mood, we have a chorus of trim young men and scantily clad girls of substantial sexual availability, not to mention the faintly sinister midget who appears in the sequence to offer advice and encouragement. One senses the beginning of a directorial talent taking over from that of the enterpreneur, though it tends to become excessively reminiscent of a hundred war movies in "Remember My Forgotten Man" the finale of *Gold Diggers of 1933*.

The sequences in *Wonder Bar*, a later Berkeley effort, are disastrous, especially the clumsy "Going To Heaven On A Mule", an unappetising rehash of every "Happy nigger" cliché from vaudeville's declining years, but in his early films his work has a control and complexity which makes it miles ahead of that engineered by his main rival, Bobby Connolly. *Footlight Parade* is his triumph. "Honeymoon Hotel" is perhaps too obvious, but "By A Waterfall" gives us an aquaballet of astonishing scope. Patterns of interlocked thighs are ploughed aside to reform as delicate filigrees, snowflakes and circles, all the time kept under control by Berkeley's skilful editing. Best of all, however, is "Shanghai Lil", which Berkeley and Bacon weave neatly into the narrative. From the moment when James Cagney, pushed by the drunken star of his show, tumbles on stage, glances around, then surreptitiously gestures to the orchestra to begin playing, the pace never falters. Long tracking shots around the Chinese bar, keyed to the music, give us some beautiful images, the best of them an opium den in which lazy eyes and half-naked bodies shift and dissolve in wreathing smoke. There is a superb bar-room brawl, some Keeler-Cagney dancing, then the usual extravaganza with marching patterns of soldiers shifting into pictures of the NRA eagle and a portrait of Roosevelt. The organisation of "Shanghai Lil" is that of a feature director, and it is not surprising that Berkeley soon switched from dance numbers to complete films. In all but their show business background they vary across a wide range, but few of them come up to the standard of the better numbers which he engineered for Warners in the golden era of the musical.

Not all technicians wished to make the transition to director, and aside from a short documentary made during the Second World War, cinematographer **GREGG TOLAND** never tried. By the manipulation of light and intelligent collaboration with the director, he was able to impose on his films a visual signature at least as distinctive as that of any other person involved. That the look of these films is attributed mainly to the director is one of the great injustices of the cinema.

Toland was, like Berkeley, a Goldwyn protégé, and it is to this producer's insight in allowing Toland through the Thirties to conduct optical experiments while in his employ that we owe much of the quality of Hollywood camerawork in the Forties. One of the first cameramen to see the importance of working with lenses and light balance to counteract the lack of sensitivity in film stocks, he developed during the middle Thirties elements of the "high key" lighting which which was to become the norm for decades after. More sensitive film hardened the image in the Forties, but the overall glow and shadowless illumination which one sees in *We Live Again* (1934), *The Wedding Night* (1935) and *These Three* (1936) is a precursor of the typical post-war style.

As Toland's mastery of light became more assured, he moved ambitiously into experiments in composition, working with unusual and oddly placed light sources, in cramped areas and from unconventional angles. His "deep-focus" style, seen to advantage in *Citizen Kane* and the Wyler films of the Forties, was more a result of his experiments in composition than lighting; as soon as faster films and more accurate lenses had been developed, the techniques followed naturally, and are in fact presaged by his highly atmospheric high and low angle shooting of *Dead End* (1937). Although Toland will be remembered for the melodrama of his looming and complex compositions for Welles and Wyler, his skilful juggling of vast light sources and balance of rich overall illumination in *Ball Of Fire*, *The Best Years Of Our Lives* and *The Bishop's Wife* are probably of greater interest and importance to the development of modern cinematography.

Equally influential as an innovator in his own field, **JACK PIERCE** exercised a control over the art of creative make-up which few men have since equalled. Chief of make-up design at Universal during its years as leader in the horror film, he created the Frankenstein monster, Mummy and Wolf Man characters with such skill that no later technician has been able to improve on them. Still under patent by Universal, these designs are among the best known examples of Hollywood skill in the combination of reality and imagination. Karloff's make-up for *Frankenstein* and its sequels is especially dramatic, but each detail was added by Pierce only after painstaking research. Reading of the ancient Egyptians' custom of binding the arms of condemned felons so as to make them stretch grotesquely after death, he gave Karloff long dangling limbs which seem terrifyingly appropriate to his distorted head. The plugs jutting from each side of the neck are a masterly touch; the monster is, as Pierce points out, basically a machine, with lightning as its motive power, so some input contact must exist.

The lumbering gait and heavy build of actors playing The Mummy in remakes of Karl Freund's classic have devalued the skilled mime developed by Karloff in the original film. In contrast to Frankenstein's monster, Imhotep, the Mummy, was conceived by Karloff and Freund as a threatening but restrained, even graceful creature, almost part of a dream. The parallel which first occurs to one is with Conrad Veidt's somnambulist in *The Cabinet of Doctor Caligari*, and Pierce's make-up adhered closely to this vision. One seldom sees the full-length mummy in the original film, and close-ups of head, shoulders and hands suggest a fine-boned sensitivity. The rotting bandages lightly cover the body in a layer of fine gauze, leaving the face and eyes relatively unobscured so as to take advantage of Karloff's saturnine features. The coating of a flaking clay-like material over the face is often all that reminds us we are looking at a creature thousands of years old, but it is more than enough. Sophisticated though make-up has become today, there are few men who approach either in technique or imagination the work of Pierce.

It is an index to the variable technical development of Hollywood in the Thirties that the make-up of Jack Pierce was more creative than most of the film music then being written. Sound in general was used in as minor a capacity as possible, and music was for the most part employed only as a backdrop to romantic comedies. Occasionally creative uses occur — the scratchy record of "In The Good Old Summer Time" which Marie Dressler plays while nodding off in her dingy room in Clarence Brown's *Anna Christie*, Dietrich strutting in black feathers to a ragtime tune at the end of *Shanghai Express* — but in general film music was in the Thirties a poor relation. It is to **MAX STEINER** more than any other man that we owe its present status as a creative part of the cinema, though we may also lay at his door some blame for the overwhelming banality of much that is foisted on us.

Steiner, staff composer at RKO for many years, departed from the conventional practice of arranging library music which surged up during action passages and disappeared when there was dialogue to be delivered. His films are scored, almost always for large orchestra or string ensemble, and make clever use of well-known tunes, popular classics and folk songs to heighten their effect. One of the first Steiner scores to gain recognition for its worth was that written for Gregory La Cava's *A Symphony Of Six Million* (1932), in which pop tunes of the time were woven into the structure. The use of "The Minstrel Boy" in *The Informer* (1935) is also skilful, evoking the purity of intent which pervaded Irish nationalism, and Steiner's Academy Award for this score is well deserved. It is an interesting index of Steiner's coarsening talent that another of his Academy Awards, for John Cromwell's *Since You Went Away* (1944), went to a score where the use of familiar tunes had taken over almost entirely. The opening shot, intended to establish that Claudette Colbert's husband had gone into the Army, leaving her with a young family, was a slow pan over an empty room against which Steiner offered us, in quick succession, a few bars of "Together", "The Wedding March", Brahms' "Lullaby", and "You're In The Army Now".

Relentlessly illustrative, Steiner's music is nevertheless effective in assisting the pace of direction and in underlining effects. The jungle crescendos of his score for *King Kong* are crude but appropriate, while his funereal title march for *The Informer* prepares us for the gloomy nature of the tragedy to follow. *Gone With The Wind* is surely the perfect "big picture" score. Here we have the simple A-A-B-A theme ("My Own True Love"), popular songs of Civil War days with homespun orchestration to match, a sweeping curtain of melodramatic melody perfectly in keeping with the visual and intellectual nature of the film. One may not find it easy to listen in tranquility to Steiner's music, but taken as a component of the films for which it was written it cannot be faulted.

Set design was a field in which Hollywood produced more than its fair share of geniuses. Cedric Gibbons, Hans Dreier and Anton Grot, supervisory art directors imposing patterns of taste on both their films and the world at large, had a wide influence on the cinema, while individual designers such as Richard Day and Wiard Ihnen had the opportunity to work out more personal visions. Among the most imaginative of these was RKO's major designer during the Thirties,

VAN NEST POLGLASE. Mainly responsible for the glossy décor of the Fred Astaire-Ginger Rogers musicals, he perfected the huge brightly lit night club sets which, in one form or another, appeared in every musical for the next twenty years. His black glass floors and looping chromium-plated banisters set a style perfectly appropriate to Astaire's fashion-plate elegance, the two elements reaching complete harmony in George Stevens's *Swing Time*, that most perfect evocation of the New York never-never-land where all Hollywood musical stars live.

Polglase, however, did not restrict himself to modern décor. His period work is faultless, particularly that recalling the middle ages. Dieterle's *The Hunchback of Notre Dame* has some of the most realistic re-creations ever engineered for an American film, with crooked roof-tops and leaning shop-fronts the design of which is impeccably judged, though equally dramatic are the sets for John Ford's *Mary of Scotland*, where the décor of Mary's Scottish castle reflects perfectly the complexities of her position. His towering judges' dais in the trial scene, the painted panels of the ceilings which loom over Mary, the tortuous castle corridors with their shadowy doorways are all elements bearing directly on the nature of the film. Less comfortable in the design of conventional sets, Polglase's cobbled run-down Dublin in *The Informer* is probably his best effort at contemporary construction, but as a designer for grand occasions he has no equal.

The roster of major technicians is endless, and there is no room here to examine in depth the work of even a handful of them. Hollywood's greatest glory was its skilled artists, the men who fulfilled the plans of the directors and producers to whom the credit goes. The fact, however, that so many of these men later became directors in their own right is an indication of the talent that resided in the ranks of these "lower orders". Their natural reticence and a modern insistence on emphasising the role of the director has prevented us from better knowing the work of the creative technicians, but it is hoped that in the future their notable contribution to the cinema will be given the recognition it deserves.

9. Reputations in Eclipse

HOLLYWOOD IN the Thirties is an historical field littered with lost reputations. For every man who survived to become famous, a dozen disappeared, retired, died, taking with them their secrets. One encounters these names in writing about the period, wonders, forgets; Barney McGill, the Warners cameraman who, in early Thirties films like Lloyd Bacon's *Miss Pinkerton* (qv) betrays a grasp of deep-focus technique presaging Toland's *Citizen Kane*; William K. Howard, a director respected by technicians, famous for the films *Transatlantic* and *The Power And The Glory*, yet curiously elusive; talented actress June Lang, whose ethereal beauty in Hawks's *The Road To Glory* makes her subsequent decline all the harder to understand. A book could be written about these forgotten people alone. For this chapter, however, there is space to concentrate on only five of them, all directors, whose work, though among the best done in Hollywood, has been largely forgotten.

Most film enthusiasts have heard of **MITCHELL LEISEN** and, when pressed, can usually remember *Easy Living* ("good Sturges script"), *Lady In The Dark* ("talk about *camp* . . .") and, with a grin, Basil Rathbone being mown down by a suit of armour in *Frenchman's Creek*. He is firmly typed as one of the Thirties comedy men, and when critics write of him at all it is with the condenscension born of boredom. "Cahiers du Cinéma" sees him as nothing more than "a great *couturier*", but one has only to feel the bitter irony of *Death Takes A Holiday* or watch Carole Lombard sputtering like a firework in *Hands Across The Table* to sense that here is a major directorial talent.

Leisen was one of the few directors to graduate from costume design. Initially DeMille's costumier (*Male And Female*, etc.), he soon mastered the Paramount opulence, and was to become one of its expert directors of romantic comedy. His work exhibits a faultless sense of design, a couturier's feeling for drapery, and an acid cynicism. All of his best films deal, in some form or other, with the ridiculousness of the male-female relationship; his men are weaklings, his women emotional cannibals who humiliate and often destroy utterly their partners. Careful control of casting allowed him throughout his career to impose this vision on his work, so that the Leisen *oeuvre* is one of the most consistent in the history of Hollywood.

Leisen's first directing experience came on two films for which Stuart Walker takes the director credit, with Leisen as "Associate Director". However, looking at *The Eagle and The Hawk* and *Tonight Is Ours* (both 1933), one finds it hard to believe that the inept Walker, a hack whose *Great Expectations* (1934) is among the most embarrassing adaptations ever engineered by Hollywood, could have confected these visual delights. The latter is innocuous, but the first, a Great War story in which the talented Fredric March plays with sensitivity and great pathos the role of a commanding officer sickened by the necessity to send out to their death the young men under his command, is photographically exciting and directed in a coherent and strongly personal style.

March's gradual mental decay is dramatised in realistic terms. His eyes sink, his mouth hardens; tortured by dreams, he rises terrifyingly from the dark to stare with blind terror into the firelight, screaming about burning places. Later he sits slumped over the long mess table as his fellow officers stand to attention toasting him for killing a German ace. His suicide is shot from below the bare springs of a stripped bed — that of his observer, killed that morning — and his dead face stares down at us while, in the background, his friend (Cary Grant) walks in to discover the body.

Two other scenes are visually outstanding, and characteristic of Leisen. The first is the discovery of Voss, the ace March has shot down. Pressing through the crowd of soldiers around the body, March finds, not some hardened Junker, but a young blond boy, bare chested, his face smooth and unlined. A low shot shows him lying as if asleep while in the background a typical German forest rises against the sky, a moving image of war and its destruction of beauty. A similar feeling is evoked in the sequence where March returns to London on a brief

139

leave. At a party, attended mainly by bloodthirsty Army men reliving their victories, he sees a beautiful girl in silver. When he leaves, the girl (Carole Lombard, in an early small part) follows him. They take a cab to a park, talk, drink champagne. March pours out his remorse and hatred of the professional war-makers. "Why can't they be kind?" he says. "*I* want to be kind," the girl replies, the implication of sexual availability quite clear. Fade out. The drape of the metallic cloth over her legs, the rattling taxi, her strange dress with its impossibly high collar; everything lends to the mood of the scene, enhanced by the fact that we neither see nor hear of the girl again.

Tonight Is Ours does not have the first film's impact, though early sequences where March pursues Claudette Colbert through the enveloping streamers of a *bal masqué* finally to track her down in her apartment and begin, in an erotic haze induced by Theodore Sparkuhl's heavily diffused camerawork, to seduce her, are true to the Noël Coward original from which the film is adapted. "I want this moment to last," he says. "How long?" "At least until breakfast." The close-ups of Colbert in ruff and columbine cap are dreamily romantic, exhibiting the same photographic quality which made *Cradle Song* (1933), Leisen's next film, and his first full directing credit, so attractive. Unfortunately this religious vehicle, intended to launch the American career of Dorothea Wieck, one of Paramount's German importations, and star of *Maedchen in Uniform*, does not succeed, despite its visual beauty.

Not one of the 13 films Leisen made in the Thirties is unworthy of serious comment, but three of them deserve special attention. *Death Takes A Holiday* (1934), though flawed by an unlikely plot, is extravagant in concept and design. Fredric March, as the physical incarnation of Death spending a few days on earth to experience life for the first time, is at his best, playing the role with a combination of arrogance and childish delight. The mannered accent, monocle and pompous speech are perfectly judged. His romance with the beautiful but self-destroying Grazia (Evelyn Venable) is played out among drooping Italianate gardens, silent fountains and pools of black water. As the melancholy "Destiny Waltz" floats from a party going on in the villa, she sits by a fountain, draped in his black cloak, and talks of death and parting. It is a strange film, notable for its decoration (designed by Leisen and Hans Dreier), skating the delicate line between poetry and comedy but never quite slipping over.

There is little poetry in *Murder At The Vanities* (1934) and its comedy is of the most brutal and cynical kind. A murder mystery set backstage at a performance of an elaborate "girlie" show, it benefits from Leisen's erotic imagination and wit. The production numbers alone would make the film worth while — semi-nude showgirls cuddling on giant powder puffs, Kitty Carlisle swimming in a "sea" of undulating plumes waved by a carpet of girls — but Leisen injects his own ideas into them. Gertrude Michael is murdered in a number called "Marahuana"; with a background of sadophallic cacti, and a chorus line of girls dressed as Mexican peons, she moans of how, when her lover is gone, she must take "sweet Marahuana" and be reunited with him in her dreams. At the climax, a man with a machine gun mows down the entire *corps de ballet*. The curtain goes down, and it is found that, under cover of this effect, the star has really been shot. Later, while a group of girls are posing at the rear of the stage, naked except for huge paper flowers around their waists, one screams as a trickle of blood from above dribbles down her breasts. Its source is the stabbed body of a private eye hidden under the web of ropes which operates the curtain. The fact that the detective is female provides another characteristic touch of Leisen bitterness.

Leisen's third great film of the period, and his masterpiece, is the underrated *Midnight* (1939), one of the best comedies of the Thirties. The Billy Wilder/Charles Brackett script is typically disenchanted, and Leisen obviously found agreeable the story of a beautiful young American girl (Claudette Colbert) who, stranded in Paris, makes a deal with an ageing aristocrat (John Barrymore) to play at being a fictitious mistress, the Countess Czerny, and thus, by jealousy, win back his wife (Mary Astor) from her lover (Francis Lederer). Everything goes well until the cab driver (Don Ameche) who loves Colbert arrives

141

at the Barrymore's country chateau determined to disrupt the plan. Claiming to be Colbert's husband, the *Count* Czerny, he settles himself in to fight.

Colbert and Barrymore counter with a telephone call which Ameche, baffled, rises from the breakfast table to answer, hearing a falsetto voice (Barrymore's) on the line announce that it is his little daughter in Hungary suffering from a bad case of measles. This failing, they put round the story that he is insane, and Colbert, moved to heights of prevarication by the situation, describes to a fascinated company how his father sent them as a wedding present one roller skate in Thousand Island dressing. There is a happy ending, but no plot twist can dispel the film's essential bitterness. Like all Leisen films, it is callous and cynical, its style faultless, its design superb. One cannot doubt that his is a major talent, sadly neglected.

The career of **GEORGE HILL** is one of the more tragic examples of waste in the history of Hollywood. An imaginative and strongly personal director, his use of naturalistic lighting and sound gives his films the unromantic surface of their best European contemporaries. After experience as a cameraman with the Signal Corps during the First World War, a unit which produced Josef von Sternberg and Victor Fleming, among others, he became one of Metro's most adventurous directors of action films. By 1930, he was respected and popular. As producer/director, he made, in collaboration with his wife, top script-writer Frances Marion, a series of highly successful films which combined, in a way seldom seen in Hollywood, keen observation with directorial style.

Min And Bill (1930), with Marie Dressler and Wallace Beery, was one of Metro's biggest financial successes, and won Dressler an Oscar for that year as best actress. Its settings, perfectly appropriate to the story of two down-at-heel inhabitants of the dockside slums and their odd relationship, are typical of Hill; intensely realistic, photographed with an imaginative use of low-key lighting, every shadow suggesting the state of mind of the central characters. This intelligent use of atmosphere was to characterise the five films Hill made in the Thirties,

142

though in *Clear All Wires* (1933) and *Hell Divers* (1932) mood was subordinate to the exposition of a conventional action story. Only in the picture of between-the-wars naval life and primitive aircraft carrier technique in the latter did either of them ever approach the peak which in his two great films of the Thirties Hill proved he could reach.

In a period infested with dramas of moral indignation, *The Secret Six* (1931) is one of the most intense. The opening shot sets its mood. Panning over the Chicago stockyards, the camera comes to rest on "Slaughter-house" Scorpio (Wallace Beery) crushing the skulls of steers with an expertly wielded sledgehammer. Leaving the abattoirs, he meets scar-faced Ralph Bellamy and goes with him to a sleazy cafe for "a hunka steak". There he eyes off Bellamy's plump, pasty blonde, listens to his tales of the pickings of organised crime, and decides to join the gang. It is the beginning of a career which is eventually to make him top gangleader of the city, ruling unchecked until a vigilante committee—The Secret Six of the title—wipes him out with the help of crusading newsman Clark Gable.

The plot of this film is largely irrelevant. There are, in fact, two stories, one a romance between Gable and Jean Harlow complicated by their involvement in the rackets, the other an attack of public apathy towards organised crime. Hill's interest in the former is desultory, but he manages in his attention to the mechanics of bootlegging to suggest the festering corruption which it bred. This is the least romantic of all the Thirties crime melodramas. The grimy rooms these people frequent and Harold Wenstrom's scabrous lighting make them seem bloodless and grub-like. The illicit still, shown in conventional gangster movies as an efficient, clinical installation dispensing whisky like plasma is, in Hill's film, a fuming almost arcane machine secreted in a filthy cellar, its bubbling pots tended by a deaf-mute whose grotesquely distorting spectacles accentuate his rat-faced aspect. To intensify this atmosphere, Hill uses sets so crowded and small that they are virtually claustrophobic, dim, harsh lights, and, instead of background music, a flood of natural sound — horns, voices, machines, shuffling feet. The employment over the end-title not of music but the sound of a newsboy announcing the end of Scorpio's reign recalls the conclusion of von Sternberg's *Morocco*, with which *The Secret Six* is roughly contemporary, but seems here to be used with even more powerful effect.

Hill's control of naturalistic lighting and sound appear best of all, however, in his masterpiece, *The Big House* (1930). Its relentless extinction of all romanticism makes this the most horrifying of penitentiary films. Once again, Beery is well cast as the brutish king of the jail, a stupid, violent potentate lounging among his sycophants. There are, as in *The Secret Six*, a number of plots — the impending release of Chester Morris, a decent, reformed criminal, and its delay by the actions of a selfish new convict (Robert Montgomery); the beginning of a romance between Morris and Montgomery's sister (Leila Hyams); Beery's growing megalomania which culminates in a prison riot. But it is the atmosphere of prison life which demands one's attention. There is no humour, not even a great deal of the companionship which most prison films dramatise. In cramped, uncomfortable cells the convicts abrade each other's nerves until the irritation spends itself in bursts of violence.

Montgomery, cast against type but turning in a convincing performance, dramatises the process by which a selfish, tough kid is made into a criminal. The scenes of his admission to prison are clinically thorough. Measured, photographed, clothed in a shapeless uniform, he is given a brusque, disinterested lecture by the warden and ejected into Beery's "empire", with its vast *Metropolis*-like dining hall, twitching, haunted stool-pigeons, and, worst of all, the horrors of solitary. In one of the most chilling scenes in the whole of Hollywood cinema, Beery is led down to the solitary block, a narrow corridor with a few cells on each side buried deep below the prison. He is herded in, the heavy iron door bolted; the guards go away — but the camera remains on the empty corridor. As the shot is held for what seems an eternity, voices seep out into the silence. "Who's that? What are you here for?" The conversation dies. A man curses, another begins hysterically to sob, a negro voice sings . . . and all the time the camera lingers relentlessly on the tiny corridor, like some quiet corner of hell.

144

Hill's best film would have been *The Good Earth*, Metro's ambitious adaptation of Pearl Buck's novel which eventually attained release over the signature of Sidney Franklin (qv). After spending some time in China collecting background footage and authentic props, including two water buffalo, Hill began in 1934 his preparations for shooting. He was at this time however estranged from his wife Frances Marion, and this allegedly preyed on his mind. Late in 1934, he was found dead in his beach-house, apparently by his own hand. His death extinguished a great talent, its loss made all the more tragic because it was a fresh and true one, among the most promising which Hollywood had ever produced.

Less individual a thinker than either Leisen or Hill, **ROY DEL RUTH** nevertheless exhibited professional ability of the highest standard combined with a skill in the placement of the camera and the use of sets as notable as that of Wyler and Ford. He worked close to his actors, and his dialogue scenes are as exquisitely lit and directed as the best French cinema. One senses in his films a genuine involvement with the characters, an ability to note reaction and expression which may stem from his early experience as a gag-writer and director with Mack Sennett, but is more probably due to an alert mind totally in command of a superior technical virtuosity.

Most of Del Ruth's early Thirties films were done for Warners, where he adapted the shadowy fast-paced studio look to his own use. *Three Faces East* (1930) was one of the first films to exhibit the characteristic Del Ruth style. A complex spy story, it presented the sad situation of Erich von Stroheim, still at that time a major directorial talent, reduced to playing the sinister butler in an English mansion who is finally unmasked as a master spy by Constance Bennett, the British undercover agent with whom he has fallen fatally in love. Von Stroheim claims to have rewritten part of the film, to the distress of Bennett and Del Ruth, and there are hints of "The Von" in the sequence of his unpacking the bags of weekend guest Bennett, admiring her lacy lingerie, as the maids spy through the keyhole, taking the magazine from her pistol and, after laying out a nightgown, leaving a book of Shelley's poems open on her pillow. The remainder is, however, just as expertly done, refuting von Stroheim's remark that Del Ruth would "never create anything important."

Both the Thirties versions of Dashiell Hammett's *The Maltese Falcon* — William Dieterle's called *Satan Met A Lady* (1936) and Del Ruth's 1931 attempt — have been condemned as inferior to John Huston's Forties adaptation, mainly, one sometimes thinks, by critics who have seen neither. One must admit that *Satan Met A Lady* is hopelessly written and acted, though blessed with a nutty logic. *The Maltese Falcon* (1931), however, is a polished and intriguing exposition of Hammett's complex plot, far closer to the original than either of the other versions, and well played by Ricardo Cortez as Sam Spade and Bebe Daniels as Miss Wonderly. Del Ruth's habit of working close to his actors is ideal for the subject, and brings to the confrontations between Spade and Brigid just the right intensity and sexual electricity. Miles Archer is played as an ugly, vulgar ex-cop, Spade as a smooth womaniser with a few saving graces, one being his insistence on avenging the death of a friend. The characterisation and casting give this version far more verisimilitude than the Huston film, where Humphrey Bogart's decision to turn Mary Astor in does not seem especially consistent with the character as played throughout. Dudley Digges may not make as effective a Gutman as Sydney Greenstreet, but Una Merkel's Effie is perfect, while the sets, especially of Spade's spacious office, far out-distance in accuracy those of later efforts.

Taxi (1932), another of Warners' low-life dramas, featuring James Cagney as a pugnacious New York taxi-driver and Loretta Young as his new wife, gave Del Ruth the opportunity once again to go for looming compositions and intelligent lighting. A dance hall sequence, with Cagney and Young losing a fox-trot competition to an agile George Raft, is unforced and smooth, as is a scene in a night-club which begins with Cagney and Young, at their wedding supper, watching the floor show, the couple entwined in an embrace which breathes content and barely controlled desire. Realism and violence, two Warners trademarks, are employed frequently; the first in shots of the fly-infested fish café where Young works as a waitress and in the use of city sounds everywhere, even over the credits in lieu of music; the second in the cab war that involves Cagney, and the gangsterism which nearly robs Young of him. However, Del Ruth's strong visual sense indelibly marks the film's style.

The same visual signature accompanies *Bureau of Missing Persons* (1933), assisted by the camera of Barney McGill. A grab-bag of plots involving the Missing Persons Bureau of the New York Police Department, this film is notable mainly for Del Ruth's low-angle shooting around crowded offices and his excellent handling of the film's grisly humour. Demoted for insubordination, a new Bureau member, Pat O'Brien, meets the team, who suspiciously inquire if he is a "rape man", all of whom have "one-track minds." He assures them he was formerly with homicide, and is then introduced to cynical Allen Jenkins, Hugh Herbert, who continually checks the morgues for the body of a girl which seems to hold for him some unhealthy necrophilic interest, and the boss, Lewis Stone. (The "jigsaw man", their expert on assembling dismembered bodies, is not in the office at the moment.) The same theme is continued in the relationship between O'Brien and Bette Davis, a client who turns out to be wanted for murder. His method of luring her out of hiding — announcing her funeral and hoping she will come to the service — is characteristic of the film's odd air.

After his Warners contract work, Del Ruth's best films are a series of musicals made for Metro, including *Broadway Melody Of 1936* and *1938*, the latter with its historic Judy Garland rendition of "Dear Mr. Gable; You Made Me Love You." His best musical, however, is *Born To Dance* (1936), a gay, fast-moving vehicle for Cole Porter's music and Eleanor Powell's dancing. Powell, agile, fresh and sexy, whose work is as underrated as that of Del Ruth, gives *Born To Dance* the exhilarating atmosphere of the best Astaire films. Her "Swinging The Jinx Away", a vast finale shot on a battleship set, sends her through all the permutations of tap-dancing, singing and acrobatics, aided by a gangling Buddy Ebsen. Just as engaging, however, is "Hey Babe", a bouncy tune sung in the lobby of a Lonely Hearts Club by James Stewart,

Eleanor Powell, Buddy Ebsen, Una Merkel, Sid Silvers and Frances Langford, to the backing of ocarinas, harmonicas and a tin whistle. The cast is a superb one, but always on camera, always smiling freshly, breaking at the hint of a suggestion into supple, fluid movement, is Eleanor Powell, as much the spirit of the Thirties in her field as Roy Del Ruth is in his.

The work of **GEORGE B. SEITZ** has been so completely forgotten that it is probably true to say that he has no reputation at all. Researchers occasionally recall his name in connection with the days of silent serials, when he was Pearl White's favourite director, but the films he made for Metro in the Thirties are largely unknown, except perhaps for the "Hardy Family" series, of which he directed more than a dozen. Seitz's most interesting films, however, are productions like *Danger Lights* (1930), one of the earliest experiments in three-dimensional cinema and 70 mm. film, and his taut melodramas of the middle Thirties which exceed in pace even the best Warners product.

Woman Wanted (1935) is one of Seitz's best films, a fast thriller in which Joel McCrea and Maureen O'Sullivan play an iconoclastic attorney and his beautiful client allied against the gang which has framed her. Beginning almost halfway through a plot, with McCrea flirting in the middle of a trial with a girl across the airshaft (O'Sullivan) who turns out to have been condemned to death a few moments earlier, it races on with a spectacular car crash, the limousine plunging through the window of a shop to land almost on top of the camera, and a series of chases directed with energetic perfection. The pauses are as tense as the action sequences, the best of them having the fugitives, hiding in an empty hamburger stall, pretend to be the owners and serve a late supper to the hungry crooks who have been chasing them. Half thriller, half situation comedy, *Woman Wanted* surges along with manic energy. Few films of the Thirties are such riveting examples of pure entertainment.

No less entertaining but more intense in mood, *Kind Lady* (*House Of Menace*) (1935) is a disturbing adaptation of Hugh Walpole's "The Silver Mask", acted with skill by Aline MacMahon, Basil Rathbone and a smooth cast of Metro regulars. Walpole's story of a kindly spinster who befriends a pauper, then is gradually dominated and imprisoned by his sinister clan, is a particularly disturbing one, evoking feelings of helplessness which are intensified by the restrained playing and George Folsey's subtly controlled lighting. As the genteel but ruthless Henry Elcott, Rathbone exhibits just the right degree of skilfully exercised charm. His first approach to his victim, who takes an interest in a painting he has done, is perfectly judged. The casual "Buy it", half plea, half order, could not be bettered.

This is a true "horror" film, rich in the sense of impotence and the special dread of evil in familiar places. Seitz builds carefully to his points of drama, giving a shocking intensity to scenes such as that which reveals the doctor MacMahon trusts to be one of the plotters, his shoulder moving in front of the lens to obscure in a sinister blur part of her horrified face. After murdering MacMahon's maid, he comes in calmly rolling down his sleeves, his *sang froid* an effective contrast to Rathbone's rigid face, an inscrutable but terrible mask. To dispel the gloom, the "family" plays a scratchy record, and as they stand stiffly round in the darkened parlour, Rathbone's idiotic "wife" dances grinning down the stairs in a white dress and jigs out from behind the vertical shadows of the banisters into the room. The disquiet evoked by this sequence is as direct as that in the most brutal fantasy of dismemberment and death. If only on the basis of this film, George Seitz would have to be considered a director of genius. His 32 films of the Thirties, however, provide richer material still for the researcher.

LLOYD BACON had the misfortune to be director of the most popular Warners musicals featuring the dance direction of Busby Berkeley. As a result, his work over the years has been subordinated to that of his collaborator, and few people consider seriously the ninety minutes of intelligently directed comedy which precedes the Berkeley extravaganzas of the last two reels. Berkeley undoubtedly made his contribution to the cinema of this period, and is given credit for this in Chapter 8. Bacon, however, was an artist of equal and perhaps greater talent.

Originally a silent comedy actor and one of the more competent Chaplin foils, the knowledge of timing he gained from his work with Sennett shows up often in Bacon's films as director. He was one of the few men able to extract from such difficult Warners stars as Al Jolson and Joe E. Brown anything approaching a consistent performance. Jolson's work in *The Singing Fool* (1928) and *Wonder Bar* (1934) is not especially good, but Bacon's direction gives him a personality which Archie Mayo in *Go Into Your Dance* (1935) was able only fitfully to achieve. In fact, the quality of Bacon's musicals for Warners, all of them dominated in most critical comment by the contribution of Busby Berkeley, is so high that it is no exaggeration to class him as the most competent Thirties director of this genre.

Forty Second Street, *Footlight Parade* (both 1933) and *Wonder Bar* (1934) are not dissimilar in format, all of them springing from such primitive antecedents as Metro's *The Broadway Melody* (1929) and Warners' own *On With The Show* (1929), a fumbling attempt at a musical based on the same material as *Forty Second Street*. All the films are episodic, built around a central male character producing some form of theatrical entertainment, invariably under heavy economic and emotional pressure. In *Forty Second Street*, the man is Broadway director Warner Baxter, struggling against ill health to produce a successful show and recover from bankruptcy. James Cagney in *Footlight Parade* plays the producer of "prologues", miniature stage shows preceding feature films which were a brief phenomenon of the early Thirties, while Al Jolson's Al Wonder in *Wonder Bar* owns a plush Parisian cabaret of the same name. In all three films, the finale is a spectacular batch of two or three production numbers, conceived and directed by Busby Berkeley with little reference to the man in charge of the film.

These three musicals, removed from the influence of their finales, emerge as superior examples of Warners' early Thirties comedy. The seedy milieu — show business has no glamour for Bacon — is typical, the fast paced dialogue and sexual innuendo equally so. One remembers

Una Merkel in a *Forty Second Street* production number being passed along a line of chorus boys and remarking conversationally to one of them, "My, you have the *busiest* hands," a gigolo in the Wonder Bar sorting through a bundle of visiting cards before handing to his latest venerable prospect one endorsed, "You are so charming; you remind me of my mother." The polarity induced by the presence in most of them of *ingénues* Dick Powell and Ruby Keeler, who, independent of the hard-bitten executives fighting and fornicating above them, end up together at the fade, gives these films a range of involvement which makes them more likeable than the average Warners low-life drama. The ubiquitous Powell provides, incidentally, one of the better jokes in any Thirties musical. Brought in by Cagney during *Footlight Parade* as the latest "discovery" of the boss's wife, he is presented to one of the dance directors, played by Berkeley himself. The harassed Busby looks over his most regular star, shakes his head, and says briskly, "I can't use him."

Bacon's style, skilfully fluid, was ideal for these films. The long tracks of *Footlight Parade* through jammed rehearsal halls dramatise the frantic pace of Cagney's operation, as do shots of lighted buses racing through the streets while showgirls inside struggle with costumes for the next number. It is, however, in his direction of actors that he succeeded most effectively. The tough, wise-cracking Jolson in *Wonder Bar* is neatly manoeuvred to make believable the final sequence in which he places in the back of a car the body of the husband his lover has murdered and encourages the suicidal owner to drive it off a cliff, thus covering up the crime, just as Warner Baxter's strongly established desperation in *Forty Second Street* gives his frantic speech to Ruby Keeler ("You're going out a youngster but you've *got* to come back a star") a conviction not suggested by the material. Frank McHugh as the neurasthenic dance director of *Footlight Parade,* clumsily leading, in crumpled hat, suspenders and cigar, the evolutions of a chorus line; Joan Blondell, Cagney's devoted secretary in the same film, Una Merkel and Ginger Rogers in *Forty Second Street,* tough girls all, but believable and alive; these are the people whom we remember long after Berkeley's complex patterns of spreading thighs have been forgotten.

The importance of his musicals has prevented writers from examining carefully Lloyd Bacon's more modest comedy work, and also such oddities as *Moby Dick* (1930) with John Barrymore as Ahab, and *Miss Pinkerton* (1932), one of the more polished comedy/dramas turned out by Warners. Joan Blondell as a nurse investigating a murder in the gloomy mansion where she works is toughly amusing, but the combination of Bacon's skilled direction and Barney McGill's remarkably advanced camerawork is the film's important feature. The use of shadows is oppressively Germanic, distorted semi-human shapes sliding and twisting across the walls in a style reminiscent of Curtiz's *Doctor X* (qv) much of which was shot on the same sets. Effects like the collapse of the dowager suggested by the gradual loss of focus, and an early use of deep-focus in a shot of the black-coated coroner's men carrying a body down a narrow set of stairs make this film a technically advanced one for its time, suggesting that McGill may be one of the most important lost talents of the Thirties.

The five directors considered here represent no more than a handful of the technicians and creators whose work deserves far more appreciation than it currently receives. Hollywood, as Joyce remarked of Ireland, was a sow that ate its own farrow. Reputations were destroyed for as little reason as a lack of commercial staying power, technicians forgotten only because they were technicians and not considered by critics to have creativity. The obscurity into which men like those named here slipped is just another shadow in the chiaroscuro of Hollywood in the Thirties.

The Thirties did not end with a blaze of glory as had the Twenties. No massive technical breakthrough or economic upheaval eventuated to still the activity of cinema's richest period. Throughout the last years of the decade, a slow but perceptible change had crept over

152

Merkel and Ginger Rogers in *Forty Second Street*, tough girls all, but believable and alive; these are the people whom we remember long after Berkeley's complex patterns of spreading thighs have been forgotten.

There was no longer any necessity to fight for survival. The battle had been won. Cinema was on top, and was to remain so for another twenty years.

Like all periods of great invention, however, the Thirties remains with us today, distorted, magnified but recognisable still. To the stormy decade from 1929 to 1939 we owe all that is good in American cinema and much that is great in film at large. The studios, the stars, the very form of this, the most flexible of all the arts, is owed directly to the work of men like Brown and Curtiz, Goldwyn and Thalberg during the period covered by this book. Perhaps we may also lay at their door the American cinema's continuing failure fully to exploit its capabilities, but this is irrelevant. Whatever the truth of the insults heaped on Hollywood in the Thirties, its influence is indisputable. It seized brashly on the opportunities of a new art and a disordered decade to create an eccentric vision of beauty. We may no longer find this vision as true as it seemed then, but its existence is incontestable. The vivid page Hollywood in the Thirties wrote in the cinema's history can never be erased.

Index

(Major references appear in bold type)

157

158

160